SURVIVAL
Strategies For
COUPLES

SURVIVAL Strategies For COUPLES

A SELF-HELP BOOK
by
DR. JOHN WRIGHT

PROMETHEUS BOOKS
Buffalo, New York

Published 1986 by
Prometheus Books
700 East Amherst Street, Buffalo, New York 14215

Published by arrangement with McClelland and Stewart Limited
Library of Congress Catalog Card No. 85-43505
ISBN 0-87975-319-6

First published in the United States by
Prometheus Books, Buffalo, New York
Originally published in Canada by
McClelland and Stewart Limited

Manufactured in the United States of America

*This book is dedicated to my parents,
Ralph Wallace Wright and Elizabeth (Joe)
Wright, who allowed me to witness from
infancy a beautiful relationship; and to
Hélène Poitras and our two children,
Michel and Sarah. Together we have built
an intimate family.*

Acknowledgments

This book would not have been possible without the contribution of many people. Our research team of Stéphane Sabourin, Pierre Gendreau, Francesca Sicuro and Huguette Courtemanche contributed to the Couple Communication Project at Université de Montréal and provided helpful feedback at various points during the creation of the book.

Hélène Poitras, Marc-André Bouchard, Conrad Lecomte, Louis Guerette, Mireille Mathieu, Cathy Fichten, John Gainer, Linda Courey and Robert Perrault helped provide a stimulating milieu for the search for an integrated model of couple functioning. Ernest Poser, John Reid, Gerald Patterson, John Gottman, Dick McFall, Niel Jacobsen, Al Marlatt, George Bach, Aaron Beck and Helen Kaplan provided many of the pieces of the puzzle. Grants from the Québec Ministry of Education and le Conseil Québécois de Recherche Social permitted our research teams at McGill and Université de Montréal to study more than two thousand couples.

I would also like to thank the more than two hundred graduate students and professionals who offered their precious enthusiasm and services during ten years. Carol Smith and Caroline Miller carefully edited the original manuscript. Louise Jobin was invaluable during the typing of this manuscript and Elizabeth Doucet helped coordinate all the many actors.

My agent, Janet Adams, provided invaluable advice and encouragement. Finally I thank my intimate partner, Hélène, for providing an amazingly stimulating and secure intimate relationship, which permitted the birth of the book.

Contents

So You Want Your Relationship to Survive

Perhaps you are a newcomer to the land of "couple" books. If so, welcome! If, however, like many people, you have already read numerous self-help books on intimate relationships – guides to healthy communication and fighting skills between partners, for example, or books on the themes of divorce, sex, child-raising and loving – you may well ask, why another "how-to" book for couples?

Here's why: in my fifteen years as a couple consultant and researcher, I have often wanted to recommend a handy reference book to couples I have helped. Every work I have come across, though, has had important shortcomings. One obvious defect is the tendency to oversimplify. Authors try to convince us that a couple's happiness depends on one solution only, whether it be effective fighting, effective lovemaking, conquering the fear of intimacy or communicating honestly and directly. I am convinced that to create a successful intimate relationship, partners must master *many* skills to resolve difficulties.

This book does not recommend that you practise the fine arts of fair fighting, listening and loving all in the same conversation or all in the same day, for different situations demand different strategies and skills. Some problems can be resolved by skillful fighting or negotiation, others by expert loving or listening. This book teaches you eight strategies to adopt at crucial points in your relationship; it also helps you decide when to use each one.

In the course of my work, helping couples improve their relationships, I have met an extraordinary range of partners.

Especially intrigued by the happy couples, my colleagues and I spent many hours interviewing, listening and watching the partners interact to discover the secrets of their success.

I have also seen many desperately unhappy couples in great distress before, during or after altercations or divorces. To help these people, and to help other troubled partners help themselves, I have directed a project that has taught more than two hundred couples how to take concrete steps in their relationship to avoid irreversible damage. All these professional experiences have led me to maintain that crucial to any effort to understand or help a couple is the belief that knowledge gained and advice offered will have a positive effect on the relationship.

Survival Strategies for Couples not only helps people understand their intimate relationships but also provides clear, commonsense suggestions for changing aspects of relationships and increasing harmony. It offers two types of information: the first will help you better understand intimate partnerships through getting to know the real-life problems couples face, their actions toward each other, their thoughts and feelings. The second type of information will allow you to examine the beliefs or myths our society encourages that seriously reduce the chances for a couple's survival. For each irrational or misguided notion, a more constructive or effective alternative is presented. As well, a precise way of analyzing how two intimates interact will lead you to become more aware of the strategies you and your partner employ. A series of tests enables you to discover more about your own relationship; to create your own couple-survival profile; to judge the fairness of your fights; and to determine how equitably you and your partner divide up the household labor.

Survival Strategies for Couples contains two additional ingredients. First, I include eight survival strategies. There are certain clearly definable ways of tackling common problems that couples encounter. Each skill is presented in an easy-to-follow, step-by-step format. In addition, you will learn how other couples have mastered the techniques. As well, I show how to change old patterns and to adopt couple-survival skills.

10

You can alter your patterns or negative behavior toward your partner and you will be shown ways to replace destructive patterns with constructive couple-survival strategies.

This book does not answer all questions, nor does it solve all mysteries. No book can. It simply and firmly maintains that the eight couple-survival strategies described are the most important routes to improving intimate relationships. It also acknowledges that each couple is unique, that no couple is easy to fully understand or explain and that every intimate relationship is mysterious.

Yet this mystery and couple-survival strategies for improving life between two partners are not incompatible.

Partners who say, "I won't read this book because it will take away the mystery from our relationship" might well ask themselves whether reading a book on how to play the guitar will lessen your awe at Segovia or at Eric Clapton's playing of the instrument. Does knowing that the combination of a sperm and an egg may result in birth diminish your appreciation of a newborn child?

The Survival Strategies

Jim and Betty,* who have been married for eight years, realize they are talking to each other less and less. Conversation, sex and leisure activities have all become dull.

Karen and Rubin, after four years together, are fighting more and more about love and lovemaking; both feel short-changed in and out of bed.

Bob, after three years of marriage, is painfully aware that he is unable to postpone ejaculation during sex, and Debbie has not reached a climax in more than a year.

Ginnie and Len are seeing too little of each other. Both have full-time jobs and find they scarcely have any time for fun, for their two children or for themselves.

*Where clinical sketches and actual dialogues are reported, names and other identifying material have been carefully modified to protect the couple's right to confidentiality.

Susan and Conrad have violent arguments at least once a day, but their fights fail to resolve their problems.

Hank and Sheila regularly engage in name-calling and dish-throwing, until Sheila ends up in an emergency department, black and blue, and Hank finds himself at the police station.

At her husband Wayne's insistence, Fay agrees to experiment with open marriage. Much to her surprise, she falls in love with a colleague at work; Wayne becomes very jealous.

Phyllis, after one year of individual psychotherapy and six sessions of couple consultation, tells her free-spirited mate, Milton, that he must choose between a monogamous relationship with her and divorce.

All these couples are facing problems common to modern relationships, and in the following chapters you will get to know them. They all confront problems that seriously threaten their chances of staying together. Each couple could call it quits by separating or divorcing. Instead, they want to continue living together even if at present they share no happiness. All have chosen to participate in a project designed to evaluate and increase couples' survival chances.

It is more difficult to survive in an intimate relationship today than ever before. Yet, although each intimate relationship is unique, most couples do face a definable set of obstacles to survival and satisfaction. What distinguishes the survivors from the non-survivors is less the kind of problems they face than the way the problems are tackled. Certain tactics, "ineffective couple strategies," employed by intimate partners will doom a relationship to failure; other tactics, "couple survival skills," will greatly enhance a couple's chances of survival.

All of the relationship histories are taken from man-woman couples. However, I have also taught couple-survival strategies to gay partners, and I am convinced that the skills can improve the survival chances and quality of a homosexual or heterosexual relationship. The skills apply equally well, too, to married couples and couples in the romantic-courtship phase, people who have not yet made the commitment to live together or to marry. In addition, the material will better equip those who are either looking for a partner or in a relationship that does not involve much commitment.

A Couple Checkup

All of us are accustomed to checkups. Dentists suggest that adults have their teeth examined once a year, children twice yearly. Many companies require that their staff get annual physicals and lung x-rays. Gynecological yearly checks are commonplace. Even automobile owners have a preventive winter checkup in the hope of saving time and money.

Most couples value their marital happiness more than they value their physical health or the smooth functioning of their automobile. But the notion of a couple checkup is still relatively new. This is partly because the definition of a happy or distressed relationship is somewhat nebulous: it depends enormously on the opinions of the two partners. What some might judge as paradise others might perceive as boring or stressful. Moreover, solutions for couples in the throes of intense conflict or for couples who want to prevent disaster have been developed only in the past twenty years and are only now being made available to the general public.

Fortunately, couple checkups do exist. You can, if so inclined, fill in the following shortened version of a survey that will give you a rough idea of the types of questions included in a couple checkup. A complete checkup would include written questionnaires like the "Couple Survival Test" on page 14, and also interviews and direct observation, by a couple consultant, of the two partners' interactions.

The Couple Survival Test

You must decide whether each statement describes your relationship. If a statement does generally describe your relationship, circle T for true, if it does not, circle F for false. You will likely find that some questions will be partially true and partially false, but you must choose the one answer that most closely describes your relationship. Instructions on how to score follow the test.

1. I feel that I can talk fairly easily about strong positive or negative feelings with my partner. T F
2. My partner often does not listen to me when I describe my feelings. T F
3. I often criticize my partner for things he/she did not do. T F
4. I tell my partner I love him/her or appreciate him/her several times a week. T F
5. At times I or my partner becomes explosively angry with little warning. T F
6. We regularly (at least once a month) have discussions lasting at least thirty minutes, in which we attempt to solve our problems. T F
7. In the past year, we have seldom discussed our feelings about our sexual relations. T F
8. We are both fairly satisfied with the distribution of housework. T F
9. We have had honest discussions about how each feels about extramarital sex. T F
10. We have regular disagreements (at least twice a month) about the amount of work one of us does outside the home. T F
11. When we have a difference of opinion about how to solve a given problem, we seldom find a compromise. T F
12. If I want to give my partner the feeling that I care for him/her, I know what to say. T F
13. When we try to solve the problems we face as a couple, we often end up discussing many different difficulties in the same conversation. T F
14. When we have sexual relations, I have an orgasm at least half of the time and so does my partner. T F
15. When we have a fight, we usually make up within twenty-four hours. T F

16. My spouse and I have important differences of
    opinion on sexual relations with others.   T F

Beside each number below is the answer that would give your
relationship a better chance of survival. If you chose a "correct" answer, enter a plus in the blank by the number; if you
choose the other response, give yourself a minus. Then add up
the pluses and subtract from them the total number of minuses
to arrive at your score.

Question Number	Best Survival Response	Refer to Chapter
1	T	3 (self disclosure)
2	F	3 (active listening)
3	F	6 (problem-solving)
4	T	4 (love)
5	F	8 (fighting)
6	T	6 (problem-solving)
7	F	5 (sex)
8	T	10 (work)
9	T	11 (open marriage)
10	F	10 (work)
11	F	7 (negotiation)
12	T	4 (love)
13	F	6 (problem-solving)
14	T	5 (sex)
15	T	9 (fight)
16	F	11 (open marriage)

Total positive _____

Minus Total negative _____

Total score _____

The more points you score higher than zero, the better are
your chances of survival. The lower your score, especially if it
is less than zero, the more likely it is that your relationship is in
distress or will experience serious conflict. Couples with very
low or negative scores need not become unduly alarmed,

however: your subjective level of satisfaction with your relationship is more important than the findings of any test. Moreover, if the low test score agrees with your opinion of your relationship, there are steps you can take to improve your situation.

No test is foolproof. The most useful purpose of this one is to underline where you and your partner are strong on survival skills and where you are weak. The right-hand column of the test refers you to the chapter that discusses the particular survival skill involved in the question.

What Are the Eight Couple-Survival Skills?

One: Open communication   Many of us hope that an intimate relationship will allow us to take off our masks, to show who we really are and to be understood and respected for who we are. Chapter Three describes how couples can effectively talk about themselves and their innermost feelings, and how each partner can encourage his/her mate to do the same. Couples will learn how to actively listen and how to avoid the pitfalls that prevent honesty and openness in a relationship.

Two: Expression of love and caring   The majority of adults hope to form an intimate relationship in which they can give and receive love. However, it is not easy to know what each of us means by "love" or to know what will make us feel loved. Chapter Four suggests strategies couples can adopt to enhance their ability to express love and to prevent the slow deterioration in loving behavior that often occurs with time.

Three: Sex and sensuality   Many couples believe that sexual compatibility and satisfying sexual relations are the key to a rich, intimate partnership. However, as many as 50 per cent of North American couples report longstanding sexual difficulties; close to 100 per cent report temporary dissatisfaction. Chapter Five describes six of the most frequent sexual problems men and women encounter. It explores the main causes of sexual difficulties and outlines several techniques couples can master to enhance their sexual relations.

Four: Problem-solving   Any intimate relationship is bound to encounter problems at some point. Chapter Six pinpoints strategies couples follow that make problems worse. It then provides straightforward guidelines for making problem-solving easier. These skills, when learned, also permit partners to find the best solutions for their difficulties.

Five: Negotiation and compromise   Most couples are bound to have differences of opinion on certain matters: about how to behave; about what to value; and about how to resolve conflict. These differences may be swept under the rug by "doves" or may cause constant bickering between "hawks." Both approaches inevitably lead to frustration. Chapter Seven shows how partners can master the art of negotiating effective compromises.

Six: Fair fighting   "Dove" couples avoid fighting altogether. "Hawks," on the other hand, fight at any and every occasion. Chapter Nine shows why it is less dangerous to fight than not to fight. It describes how to learn to fight fairly, and analyzes (with excerpts from case histories) the various strategies employed by "dove" partners, "hawk" partners and fair fighters. Then the tactics adopted by "dirty" fighters are compared to those that will permit clean, constructive fights.

Seven: Division of work   The division of labor in a modern family is far more complicated than ever before. Couples can feel they have failed if they assume the "traditional roles" (one partner employed outside the home, one responsible for the housework), but they can also feel they have failed, for different reasons, if they adopt the dual-career option. Chapter Ten presents ways to help couples decide what distribution of out-of-home and in-home work best fits their situation. As well, several solutions are given to the common problems of unequal distribution of work within the home and how long hours on the job can keep one partner away from home responsibilities.

Eight: Sexual openness and independence Increasingly, couples are engaging in sexual relations outside the principal partnership. Discord about extra-conjugal relations is one of the most frequent causes of stress in intimate relationships. However, monogamy is no cure-all. Chapter Eleven presents the eight essential questions couples can discuss in deciding whether to pursue a monogamous or an open relationship. It also includes several examples of couples who attempted both options.

Should we separate and, if so, how? Many couples must decide whether to separate. Chapter Twelve examines the basic questions partners can ask themselves in attempting to reach such a decision. It explores the various options open to partners, from parting to resuming "business as usual." In addition, it provides suggestions on the kinds of separation that will minimize damage to partners and to their children.

Before trying to learn the eight survival strategies, many couples have found it helpful first to better understand two crucial questions confronting modern couples. Why is it harder for intimate relationships to survive? And what is love? Many couples find that only after these two questions have been answered are they ready to invest the energy required to learn the survival strategies. Without answering these questions, nagging doubts can undermine a partner's motivation to improve the relationship through the survival-skills approach.

If you feel you have already answered the questions to your own satisfaction, then feel free to skip the next two chapters and start work on improving your survival strategies immediately.

18

1

Why Are Intimate Relationships So Difficult?

Is it really more difficult today than it used to be to maintain a stable, intimate relationship? According to divorce statistics, it is. Between 1960 and 1980, the divorce rate in Canada increased by 500 per cent. Every year, marriages on the average are lasting for fewer years, and millions of dollars are spent annually on divorce lawyers' fees. At the present rate there will be as many divorced individuals as married individuals by the year 2000.

Why are more intimate relationships ending in separation and disillusionment? Are such relationships worth the time and effort we put into them, or should we just give up on them as relics from a past era? Is there anything we can do to improve our own intimate relationship other than crossing our fingers and hoping we do not become part of the divorce statistics?

Why Separation Rates Are Rising

One: Rising expectations – marriage as the cure-all Modern couples expect more from marriage than their predecessors. Earlier generations expected marriage to offer them the chance to have children and the opportunity to build a home in which both partners could grow old together. In the past twenty years, however, spouses have come to expect their partners to supply them with a much longer list of benefits, from children and financial security to friendship, housework, home repairs and sexual pleasure. Yet, it is not clear whether we are willing or able to do what is required to achieve these larger aspirations. While we are demanding more from marriage, two other attitudes that our parents held remain with us. Like them, we believe that we are born with the ability to form a fulfilling marriage, and that good marriages happen, they are not built.

Two: Changing sexual attitudes Our culture now talks openly about sexuality; indeed, we are constantly bombarded by sexual stimuli in the media. One positive outcome is that a great deal more is now known about sexual adequacy and inadequacy. Simultaneously, however, many people have raised their sexual aspirations to an unrealistic level. Couples today increasingly complain of sexual difficulties. As well, with the "sexual revolution" has come the temptation to fulfill sexual needs outside the primary relationship. Many partners, instead of resolving sexual conflict with their mates, seek pleasure with new partners. One result has been open marriage, which, while solving some problems, creates many new ones.

Three: Changing roles for men and women Previous generations found it relatively easy to decide who would do what in a marriage: the woman would look after the house, raise the children and give affection and support; the man would be the breadwinner, initiate sex when he wanted it and, if necessary, discipline the children. This separation of roles in "traditional" marriages is slowly losing favor in western cultures. Changes in the job market and in child-rearing practices and broader educational and career opportunities for women are altering traditional definitions of men's and women's roles. Not surprisingly, therefore, intimate relationships between men and women have also undergone some transformation.

These changes have led to more flexibility in the behavior of the sexes. As a consequence, modern couples face questions their parents never needed to consider. Who will do the housework? Who will raise the children? Who will make the financial decisions? Whose career takes priority? How shall we express affection? How will we depend on each other? How independent can we be yet remain committed? Can we show our weaknesses and not jeopardize the relationship?

Many couples find that, if they do not formulate satisfactory answers to these questions, their relationship will be stricken with conflict and dissatisfaction.

Four: Less parental support Fewer couples can depend on their parents for the things previous generations could. The tight, extended family proved invaluable for moral, financial and social support during the highly stressful events of marriage, illness, childbirth and conflict. Nowadays, with the increased mobility of couples, higher separation rates and the lower value placed on the extended family, couples are left to face their problems alone.

Five: Changing divorce laws In North America, it is much easier than before to separate when a relationship is no longer working to either partner's satisfaction. Previously, only malevolent or illegal acts – physical or mental cruelty such as adultery and nonconsummation – were accepted by the courts as grounds for divorce. Today, the law is more accommodating, and couples in unworkable relationships can choose to separate rather than suffer together as previous generations did.

Six: More accepting attitudes toward divorce Once, divorced people were regarded as failures, monsters or losers; they are now accepted as normal, worthy human beings. Why the turnabout? Society has had no choice but to change its attitude. As we witness half our friends and family separate, how can we continue to believe that only the sick or inadequate divorce? One inevitable result of society's acceptance of marriage breakdown is that many partners, dissatisfied with their relationships, are now much less hesitant than were their predecessors to separate.

Seven: The "me" generation Our parents were raised to sacrifice individual needs for the good of family, community and country. Recent generations have been exposed more to the values of self-expression, self-growth, sexual awareness and personal freedom. Whereas our parents found it natural to work long hours every day for many years so that each partner and the children could be happy and secure, modern couples are much less willing to make sacrifices. Today's "me" generation has found freedom and satisfaction in the sexual, educational and social spheres that our parents never dreamed of. Nevertheless, one question still begs an answer: has this generation succeeded in satisfying individual needs, even at the expense of satisfying the needs of intimate relationships?

How to Make Sense of the Overall Situation

None of the seven causes outlined above works in isolation. They combine to produce the changes we witness in intimate relationships; they also influence how long these relationships will last. Thus, couples now experience more stress; yet they have no special skills to cope with it and they find less support from their families and society than did previous generations.

The stress factor alone could explain why couples separate more often: they experience less pleasure from their relationships because of the amount of stress relationships must withstand. Previous generations might have tolerated a stressful or unpleasant relationship if they were daunted by the threat of legal action or moral censure. For modern couples, however, there is little to deter them from ending an unsatisfactory relationship. The partner who feels dissatisfied with her/his relationship will receive a good deal of support from all quarters when she/he explains: "I am leaving my relationship because *I* am no longer satisfied with it."

Yet, we often terminate a relationship without making a sustained effort to improve it, although it might have been salvageable with some work by both partners. (Chapter Twelve discusses this issue.)

Are Intimate Relationships Worth the Hassle?

Because this generation sets such value on the satisfaction of individual needs and because divorce statistics are steadily rising, you might expect individuals to value love relationships less than they once did. But no such trend has been noted. Satisfaction from a stable, intimate relationship is still regarded as the greatest joy in life by most North American adults; and marital distress and marital separation are still rated by them as the greatest sources of pain and stress. With joy and anguish in the balance, then, we might well ask whether intimate relationships are worth all the effort. The answer for the majority of adults in western cultures is an unwavering yes. So, what are the pleasures that intimate relationships promise and deliver, however fleetingly, for some couples?

Feeling loved: Love means many things to many people, but most agree that it is a feeling difficult to forget. To feel loved and appreciated by another person can be one of the most treasured experiences of a lifetime.

Feeling understood: In this technological age of high stress and increased social isolation, we can feel amazingly warm and comforted when another adult gets to know and understand us.

Feeling accepted: With pressures all around us to produce, to achieve and to improve, it is wonderful to hear someone who knows us intimately say, "I love you and accept you."

A hedge against stress: Human existence inevitably involves many challenges and stresses. Studies have consistently shown that those who receive support from an intimate relationship more readily overcome them and better survive the crises of illness, unemployment, political strife and aging.

Children: For some couples conceiving, giving birth and raising children are the most gratifying of all life's experiences.

Sexual expression: More and more people aspire to full sexual expression with another adult. The anxiety and challenge of the seduction phase of a brief relationship can be very intense; but many forms of sexual expression are only feasible and truly exciting if each partner knows the other's physical and emotional needs. Such understanding is usually only possible if the relationship is a stable one that has endured for some time.

A place called home: Most human beings strongly desire a place of their own, where they can relax, sleep, work or play. Whether the territory is owned or rented, temporary or permanent is often of less importance than whether it is shared with a partner.

Improving the Quality of Your Relationship

Couples can take action to improve the quality of their relationships; I call this active approach the "couple survival-strategy perspective." I have found that if partners are willing to take an honest look at certain beliefs they hold and at certain ways in which they act, impressive changes are possible.

Each of the following chapters will help you identify key beliefs and behaviors. You will learn which ones can wreak havoc on intimate relationships. Realistic expectations are carefully defined, along with guidelines to help you change old patterns and behave more effectively toward your partner.

One advantage to this approach is that instead of passively watching their relationship deteriorate, a couple can actively take steps to improve their partnership. A second advantage is that the survival-strategy perspective allows couples to learn specific procedures to improve their relationship. It debunks such fatalistic myths as: "You are born with the ability to be a successful intimate partner" or "A successful relationship simply depends upon choosing the right partner."

Last, but not least, the survival-skills approach does not treat all couples as if they were identical. On the contrary, individual differences are respected, accepted as both natural and beautiful. Consistent with this notion is the belief that once two people have learned some of the survival skills, they and they alone choose which skill to apply and how to apply it.

As anyone who has been involved in an intimate relationship will appreciate, survival skills must be approached realistically. There are no surefire guarantees that, if you apply all the skills described in this book, your relationship will survive: as you know, lasting happiness between intimates is infinitely complicated and mysterious; no single set of skills can hope to fathom it.

A good deal of couple satisfaction depends upon the compatibility of the partners, and survival skills cannot overcome certain crucial incompatibilities. Moreover, as individuals change with time, so do their needs; two individuals who were once complementary can eventually drift apart. While the survival skills will help certain couples grow closer together, others would be better advised to undertake a constructive separation rather than continue in a destructive relationship.

Couples who master the problem-solving, negotiation and fair-fighting strategies are far better able to achieve a constructive separation if they do decide to end their partnership. While the strategies may not have helped the couple stay together, they certainly enable each partner and the children to part with less pain.

There is no magic couple-survival formula. Couples must learn new ways to conceptualize intimate relationships and new ways to interact in them. The task is akin to learning to speak a new language; as with any new skill, the early practice can feel awkward, clumsy and unnatural. But practice makes perfect. More than 80 per cent of the couples who have completed our survival-skills program report high degrees of satisfaction with the strategies they have mastered. As well, many partners have found the exercises to be fun and stimulating. A little of the magic and mystery may be temporarily taken out of relationships during the learning of this new orientation, but the benefits of such an innovative vision of intimate partnerships far outweigh the confusion and frustration they supplant.

2

Understanding Love

Studies have shown that "to be loved" is the strongest wish of most North American adults. "Love" is usually why we decide to marry. Death or decline of "love" is the reason most frequently cited for divorce. Despite the sometimes almost mystical powers we attribute to "love," many of us are poorly equipped to satisfy this, our strongest desire.

In this chapter, we will describe the discoveries scientists and therapists have made about love. But first, we will tackle three questions that inevitably arise at some point during an intimate relationship. What is love? How does love develop? What factors prevent the expression and acceptance of love?

What is Love?

Although most of us will agree that love is of utmost importance to us, it is unlikely that we'll agree on any of love's characteristics. Neither lovers nor scientists can easily define love. To demonstrate the complexity of the concept, try to complete the following statements with a few words:

1. I think love is _____.
2. My partner thinks love is _____.
3. At the beginning of our relationship, I thought love was

   _____.

4. At the beginning of our relationship, my partner thought love was _____.

Ask your partner to carry out the same exercise; then compare your answers. You will probably find that your ideas differ drastically from those of your partner; the contrast may be quite shocking. You will almost certainly find that your present concept of "love" differs from the view you took at the beginning of your relationship.

There are many dimensions to the concept of love. Some people interpret love as a strong personal feeling recognizable by its physical effects: a pounding heart, loss of breath or a hot flush. For others, love is strongly linked with our behavior toward a partner and our partner's behavior toward us: are we generous, caring, supportive, understanding, sacrificing or seductive in our interaction?

Some people may see love as a pattern of thoughts: "My partner protects me, is a good parent, needs me and misses me when we're not together." Some people cannot imagine love without sexual excitement: "Love is a surge of sexual attraction," or "to love is to make love." For others, love and sex are independent: "I can be strongly aware that I love my partner and that my partner loves me, whether or not I am sexually aroused." Many people associate love with the sometimes painful passion of early romance: "We felt real love when we first met. It was like lightning." For others, love is a steady, relaxed, comfortable state shared by two excellent friends.

Some believe love is only possible as long as there is risk, adventure, uncertainty and fresh experience. For others, love is reached only after many years of shared trust and understanding. We may associate love with jealousy and possessiveness: "I would die if my partner even looked at someone else." Or we may have no qualms about loving someone who is not "our own"; our love may thrive on our partner's independence.

Love may demand predictability or constant surprise, even displeasure. We may need a partner from a background similar to our own who shares our values or a partner who is our opposite. Some of us can only love someone we find physically beautiful. For others, attractiveness may be less important than intelligence, an ability to care, strength or even health.

We may know what sparked our love. We may know which of our own and our partner's characteristics and what aspects of our relationship nurture our love. Or love may be a weird and wonderful mystery.

How Does Love Develop?

Most experts agree that we are not born with an ability to give and receive affection. We develop a capacity to love during childhood, adolescence and adulthood. Four aspects of our experience influence the personality traits that attract us and the ways we convey our caring to a partner: our relationship with our parents; our relationship with our siblings and peers; our previous partners; and our present relationship.

Parents: Freud and his disciples have emphasized the parent-child relationship almost to the exclusion of other experiences as the dominant factor in our development of a capacity to love. To be able to love someone else, we must have a certain degree of self-love and self-acceptance. Proponents of the Freudian school of thought believe that self-love can only develop with parental love as its model.

If we enjoyed a stable and consistently loving relationship with our mother and father, chances are we will be able to feel strong love for a partner. If our parents encouraged us to express our feelings and if they were affectionate with each other, we will find it relatively easy to express this love. However, if our parents gave us little affection or if the affection they gave us regularly alternated with punishment or rejection, we will find it harder to love. In Freudian terms, we unconsciously seek to duplicate our first intimate relationship – our relationship with our parents – with our partners; we attempt to relive that original emotional experience by modeling our actions on behavior typical of that relationship.

Siblings and peers: Fortunately, our parents are not the only people who can teach us how to give and receive love. Studies during the past fifteen years have shown that our brothers and sisters, our friends and society in general can strongly influence our desires and expectations and our behavior in love. In fact, closeness with a sibling or peer acceptance can at times be a powerful antidote to the insecurity resulting from a difficult parent-child relationship. Many who have had a sour relationship with a parent have founded a strong and constructively loving relationship with a sibling or friend that has served as a good model for future loving.

However, if as children we felt that we had to compete with a brother or sister for our parents' affection, we might be insecure adult lovers. If we were encouraged to think that our brother or sister is better than we are, we may have difficulty trusting a partner in an adult relationship. The tendency will be to compete with our partner as we did with our sibling.

Previous partners: Our first adventures into the world of romantic love can also strongly influence our patterns of loving. If you were rebuffed by the first person you fell for, you probably needed several positive experiences to eradicate the effects of that first rejection. Adolescents tend to fall in and out of love quite easily. The rapid and extreme fluctuation between passion and despondence that we experience in adolescence is in many ways excellent training for the future. During adolescence we learn how to give and receive sensual love and we have a chance to discover a suitable "type" of partner.

The adult who has experienced an open exchange of love with others will enter a relationship with expectations very different from those of a lover who has never shared an intimate relationship with another adult. Partners who enter a new relationship after a painful separation will likely be looking for characteristics in their new mate that will prevent a recurrence of their frustration.

Our present relationship: Pleasant and unpleasant experiences in the early stages of our present relationship are also crucial. If we enjoy positive feelings and pleasant thoughts while we are with our partner, our love and attraction for him/her will remain strong. However, if we experience more unpleasantness than pleasure, our ties to our partner will weaken.

When we first fall in love, pleasurable intimacy far outweighs any unpleasantness; but this situation changes, either slowly or rapidly, for various reasons. We have all watched love in many marriages fade considerably over time, although spouses often decide to continue a "marriage of reason" once their love is gone: "For the kids"; "I wouldn't want to hurt him/her"; or "I just couldn't make it alone." Why is it so difficult to maintain love in a stable relationship? There are probably as many reasons as there are couples.

What Factors Prevent the Expression and Acceptance of Love?

Misconceptions About Love

We will concentrate on three important factors that block love: misconceptions about love; avoidance of potential emotional pain; and incompatibility. Our society has promoted a variety of beliefs that are not only irrational, but also destructive to the effective give and take of love between intimate partners.

"We were crazy about each other when we met. If only our love was as strong now as it was when we first fell in love." How many times have you heard this lament? Many couples form a stable relationship because they went through an experience that our culture labels "falling in love." This is the love that is the basis of most romantic poetry and novels. Words such as "passion," "desire," "craziness," and "worship" are all used to describe the experience. Such love often involves putting the desired one on a pedestal, so that she/he seems perfect. Once on this pedestal there is a risk that the loved one will reject us – how could we ever be worthy of such perfection? When the loved one accepts us, we rejoice, because it must mean that we, too, deserve to be on a pedestal. In the ensuing struggle between passion and reason, reason often loses; we throw objectivity, and possibly our destiny, to

the wind. We think only of our lover, happily ignoring negative attributes and exaggerating positive ones, willing to do anything to please. Our culture describes this experience as "falling in love" because of our sense of loss of control, both of our reason and our fate. Our cognitive faculties become slave to our emotions, and we see positive attributes in the loved one that objective observers cannot see.

We decide to live together, to form a stable relationship. Then, slowly for some, rapidly for others, the glow fades. We begin to notice a few unpleasant characteristics and irritating habits that had escaped our attention. Our lover's fantastic qualities shrink to more human proportions. Our mad passion for our lover grows less intense; for some of us it disappears completely. We begin to ask ourselves, "Is this all love is? Have I made a mistake? Has my partner changed so much since we married?" If we are lucky, romance will be followed by other kinds of love; if we are not, we will have nothing but, at best, pleasant memories.

Many ask, "Why let romantic love die? Why not try to keep the fires burning?" This can only be done by maintaining the conditions that were present during the romance. Think of romantic novels: war, a jealous husband, saintly wife, forbidding parents, distance or death prevented the passionate pair from enjoying more than a few fleeting moments in each other's arms. Their appetite for each other was never satisfied.

There is always a bittersweet mixture of pleasure and pain in romantic love. If partners are never able to spend much time together, they never see each other under adverse or uncomplimentary circumstances and the illusions are never broken. The loved one never comes down from the pedestal.

One of the paradoxes of romantic love is that it leads us to desire the other even more strongly: "I can't get enough of you." Therefore, romantic love can trigger the decision to form a stable relationship. After all, what could make more sense than marrying someone you can't get enough of? But the situation changes suddenly and drastically when you move in together. You can stop worrying about losing your partner:

you've signed a contract and set up house. The constant thrill of the challenge to win your partner's love is gone; now it has become easy to take her/him for granted.

What are the alternatives? There are three. One: never commit yourself to a lover. As soon as you notice that the romance is coming to an end, break it off and begin searching for a new partner. Two: tolerate the boredom of living with this dramatically changed person who used to be so much fun, who used to be such a good lover. Dwell on the memory of your honeymoon or fantasies of a potential new love. Three: gradually allow a part of your original passion to be supplanted by new kinds of love that grow out of shared experiences, trusting and helping each other, a fulfilling sex life, having children and so on.

Why do so many of us embark on a relationship based on these new kinds of love so halfheartedly? Because our culture - our songs, books, films - encourages us to value romantic love above all other love. As a result, we know little about identifying and enhancing the love that grows out of a union. Tragically, we often have little regard for a love that is not "romantic."

"If my partner really loved me, she/he would know how to make me feel loved." Many of us honestly assume that a truly considerate lover knows what we need to feel happy, that we should not have to define our needs. This assumption is particularly dangerous when made by both partners. Each sits back waiting for the other to make the first loving move, the result being a cold, inactive love life.

"We should love others in the way we ourselves want to be loved." There are about as many possible definitions of love as there are people. Some of us, however, are inclined to forget that there are ways of loving other than our own. It is likely, in fact probable, that our partner's expectations of love do not match our own.

Since our preferences in love are determined by a combination of various factors - childhood experience and relationships, environment - it is only natural that two partners won't be interested in or stimulated by exactly the same experiences.

You may protest, "But when we were courting, we seemed to like all the same things. I assumed that my partner was genuine. That is one of the reasons I chose to stay with her/him, because I like the things she/he finds stimulating."

Remember that during courtship, passion dominates reason; more is at stake, and each partner is working tremendously hard to win the other's heart. At this stage, we see a limited range of likes and dislikes. Many stalemates in loving could be avoided if, during the relationship that develops beyond courtship, we tried to learn more about our partner's preferences rather than attempting to please with what we enjoy.

"If we have chosen well, our love will last forever." Here we have another dangerous misconception, based on the assumption that the perpetuation of romantic love is guaranteed by the correct choice of partner. Undoubtedly, we match up with certain types of people more successfully than with others, and a good match of styles of loving will help a relationship to last. However, a wise choice merely prepares the garden and plants the seed. If you don't water and weed the seedling and provide sun, it won't grow. Certain skills must be exercised. An unnurtured love, like an abandoned garden, will die.

"True love will never change." Many of us think we know what to expect when we enter a relationship. He assumes that because she is seductive, affectionate and energetic now, she will always be this way. She knows that he is sensitive, passionate and a free spirit, and assumes he will always be this way no matter what happens. However, love is not static. As a couple lives together, their situation changes and so do their expectations and appreciations of each other. A woman who valued her partner early in the relationship for his unpredictability and independent spirit might, after some years, come to admire his consideration and support. After those years, a man who was initially excited by his partner's appearance and *joie de vivre* might place greater value on her intellectual capacity and moral support. Distressed people often complain

that their partners have changed; they aren't the way they used to be. Some people feel they don't know their partners any more. Through couple checkups in the survival course, we invariably find that, with time, both partners change. Not only do they approach each other differently, but their estimations of each other change. We have identified three principal causes of these changes: habituation, maturation and new demands.

Habituation: When we are presented repeatedly with the same event, a process called "habituation" takes place. Even champagne and caviar would lose their attraction if we were to indulge in these luxuries three times a day. A partner's good looks, sexual prowess or way with words, which might seem enormously attractive at the beginning of a relationship, will in time lose their potential to arouse.

Maturation: The human personality is never stagnant. We are most aware of the process of constant change in young children, but our sexual needs and our needs for emotional stimulation, stability and challenge change as we enter adulthood. A young couple may value mobility and move annually. But, as they have children, complete certain projects and achieve career objectives, it may become more important to build a life in one place. After some years of stability, a change of environment or new challenges may again be desirable.

New demands: With each phase of life and each phase of a relationship certain demands give way to new ones. The pressures felt by two partners who have no steady income but no children and few debts give way to different priorities as they launch careers, buy a home and have children.

Change is inevitable. We should therefore assume that some or even most of the characteristics that initially attract us to our partners will change. And, just as it is unreasonable to assume that our partner will like what we like, it is unreasonable to assume that the love needs of both partners will change in the same fashion. Many couples are caught by surprise when they notice after five years of intimate life that "You're not the person you used to be." However, nothing could be more natural. Couples who desire to maintain a rich give and take of love would be safer to assume that they will have to vary the love they give constantly to keep in touch with the changes in their partner's needs.

"I cannot control the love I feel, nor can I influence the way my partner feels about me." Many partners see love as a static thing. Some of us believe that our love is beyond our control and that our mate's attempts to please are arbitrary and independent of our own behavior. This myth is often supported by the Freudian theory that all important determinants of why and how we love are fixed by the time we leave adolescence. However, current research indicates that our desires and our ability to satisfy a lover's desires depend, to some extent, on how we communicate with our partner.

This implies that two people can learn to be more loving. Our communication strategies are based on the premise that we can help our lover better satisfy our emotional and sexual needs, and our partner in turn can help us satisfy his/her needs more fully. Lack of self-knowledge or lack of open communication may keep us from giving a partner the cues necessary for her/him to act in ways that will make us feel loved. We may even inadvertently reprimand our partner when he/she is actually on the right track.

"If you really love me, you will take me as I am." The "take-me-as-I-am" type of partner believes that, once a relationship is launched, all the work is done, that the other should be satisfied with the finished product: "I was born that way." "That's just the way I am." "My father was like that and so am I." "Women are like that." These and similar excuses are frequently proffered to justify a lack of motivation to be affectionate in the way our partner desires.

The idea that anyone should or could completely accommodate the inflexibility of another, which is indeed what this misconception demands, is unreasonable and, perhaps, impossible. Somewhere between malleability and rigidity is a style that enables workable compromise and an easy exchange of love and affection.

Avoidance of Potential Emotional Pain

Certain expectations reinforced by society lead us to hold irrational and inhibiting beliefs about love. These beliefs have a direct impact on how we define love, how we behave and how satisfied we are with the love we receive from our partner. They may make us reluctant to show strong feelings, to let ourselves go. We need to understand and overcome our fears of potential rejection, embarrassment, dependency or anger if we hope to reach our loving potential.

Fear of rejection: In love, we often have to be ready to go out on a limb, to take a chance on delivering what we think our partner wants. We have to be willing to take risks. When we say, "I wish you would come to bed with me," "I need a hug," "Let's take a trip together" or "Let's have a baby," we are opening up, revealing what it is that we need so we will feel loved, what will make us happy. In doing so, we run the risk that our partner will respond. "I'm not in the mood," "No, I don't want to," "I'm not interested." If our offers of or requests for love are refused often enough, we may conclude unhappily that our partner has rejected us. "You don't want what I have to give," "I can't please you," "You don't love me." If our efforts to communicate emotions or desires have been frequently disregarded by parents, peers or a previous lover, we will be very vulnerable, afraid of rejection. We may be so devastated at hearing someone say, "I don't feel like making love tonight," that we miss the "I love you" that follows.

Partners who share many positive experiences in their relationship with their children, at work or at leisure will be less threatened when their offers are declined or their requests are denied. If one says, "I'm too tired to make love," or "I can't talk now, I'm feeling a bit down" or "You're confusing me," the other will be less likely to interpret the comment as a mark of his/her own inadequacy. Partners who share few positive exchanges are much more vulnerable to the effects of rejection. They may lose interest in the relationship, become depressed and withdrawn or immerse themselves in activities outside the relationship. They may become aggressive or openly hostile toward the other partner. The situation may even degenerate to the point at which separation is the only solution.

Fear of embarrassment: Someone who believes that open shows of affection and requests for love reveal weakness or immaturity will be awkward about giving or receiving affection.

The passionate personality glorified by the Romantics was successfully quashed by the Victorians, who idealized tight control over all emotions. The western world is now a mosaic of styles of loving. Anglo-Saxon cultures, which often abhor open displays of affection, are a sharp contrast to Latin and some European cultures, which show no such aversion. North American men are often shy to show emotion in public: "My father wasn't demonstrative nor am I. It's not manly." The partner who feels no embarrassment about giving and receiving affection may wonder why her/his mate should be so reluctant.

Fear of dependence: When we become attached to another, we can come to depend on him/her not only emotionally but also for financial and physical security, and for sharing responsibilities. To love and need another leaves us open not only to the risk of rejection, but also to withdrawal of support and protection. Those who were neglected or cut off from parental protection in childhood, or who have had an unsuccessful relationship with an unsupportive partner, may feel a strong need to be protected. Or they may fear that if they allow another person too far into their lives they will again be open to the traumas experienced earlier.

Marriages of the 1950s and 1960s were more often than not based on traditional sex roles: he was the breadwinner, she the housewife. Women of this period were not afraid to depend on their husbands for financial support and protection; in fact, society expected it of them. Partners in this traditional arrangement had very different roles: the woman was expected to specialize in child-rearing and housekeeping, while her husband pursued a career outside the home. Many mothers communicated to their offspring their resentment at having been forced to "depend" on a man this way and to sacrifice a career for marriage and motherhood.

Within the past two decades, this pattern has radically changed. Increasing numbers of women have refused to be so dependent on a man and have demonstrated that they can perform as well if not better than men in careers outside the home. In many households both partners are now bread-winners. However, these contemporary women probably had mothers who may have shared love easily but who were very dependent on their partners and therefore took second place. As a consequence, some women of the 1970s and 1980s fear that complete commitment to a loved one will require that they suppress their ambition and independence.

Such an aversion to dependence can have various negative consequences. We may feel the need to maintain tight control of all feelings of love so we do not become too dependent on another. We may avoid intimate relationships completely or make only a superficial commitment without deep emotional roots.

Anger: Some of us feel that anger and love are incompatible, that we can't feel anger or resentment toward a partner and love her/him at the same time. Whether we can tolerate these two apparently incompatible feelings toward the same person depends greatly on our childhood experiences. Certain styles of parenting encourage children to be aware of their emotions and to express love and aggression simultaneously. Other styles encourage tight control or denial of anger. If our parents used the latter style we may be poorly prepared for intimacy in adulthood, for all intimate relationships are a bittersweet mixture of love and anger.

Unfortunately, some of us are so poorly equipped to deal with feelings of anger that we avoid them at all costs. We may stop before we get too close to another person, avoiding potential conflict by holding back our love. Or we may refuse to notice even the slightest fault in our partner, fearing that any anger we would express would extinguish our love. This is dangerous behavior: an exaggerated fear of expressing anger can jeopardize a relationship.

Partners who do not communicate effectively and who have accumulated unsolved problems will also harbor great frustration and anger. For a distressed couple, exchanges of hostility can become more frequent than exchanges of love. Each partner may feel so much anger that his/her own positive feelings or any loving gestures by the other go unnoticed. Once the relationship has degenerated to this extent, the couple should seek professional help to release their frustration and resolve their problems.

Incompatibility

Social scientists have devoted much attention to such questions as what initially attracts us to each other, what makes us fall in love, why we decide to get married, which personality combinations are most likely to survive and which are doomed from the start.

I have found, however, that these analyses have only moderate success. Often two people who I would never have predicted could survive as a couple do, in fact, develop a very rich and mutually satisfying relationship. Similarly, two people who seem to have everything going for them often end up on the rocks.

It is impossible to explain success or failure in a relationship in simple terms; however, motivation and interaction skills seem to be the crucial factors. Two people who look like they do not stand much of a chance can build a very satisfying relationship if it means enough to both of them. The skills necessary to build a mutually satisfying relationship can be developed; survival strategies can be planned.

Motivation and skills aside, what about compatibility? If two individuals are mismatched, disharmony will surely kill any desire to co-operate. He may be a skillful problem solver, while she is good at expressing her emotions; but what if her skill is constantly neutralized by his incompetence? What if they can never get their act together? When applied effectively, the negotiation and supportive listening skills outlined in the following chapters can conquer seemingly insurmountable incompatibilities.

Social scientists cannot agree on the personality types to form a happy relationship, but they have identified combinations of individuals who should probably not undertake marriage. If these personality types do combine in a relationship, they will need to be adaptable if they want to find happiness together.

Laswell and Lobsenz[1]* have discussed compatible and incompatible pairings in their excellent book, *Styles of Loving*. They identify six types of lovers: the best friends, the unselfish, the logical, the possessive, the romantic and the game players. Several combinations are quite promising, but others are particularly explosive.

A "possessive-lover/game-player" match is a dangerous one. The possessive lover needs to feel in complete possession and control of a partner and thrives on hours of intense contact, and will become extremely jealous at the thought of losing a lover to another. A game player may enjoy the challenge of seduction, but won't want to feel too close for too long. While the possessive lover fears rejection and craves security, a game player is afraid of dependence and predictability. Small wonder that their usually short relationships are filled with explosive conflict. Yet two possessive partners could survive together, provided each is ready to be patient with the other and to take the necessary steps to satisfy the other's insecurities.

The combination of two romantic-style lovers is another explosive match. Staying "in love" indefinitely presents significant problems. Each partner must keep the other permanently on a pedestal. Diehard romantics will want to maintain an idealized image of their partner at all costs. Disillusionment may bring accusations of deception: "You falsely led me to

*Each number in the text corresponds to a numbered reference in the Bibliography, p. 231.

40

believe that you were . . . ." An unwillingness by both partners to accept the less appealing aspects of each other's personality will likely lead to each "falling out of love" with the other, often accompanied by intense accusatory battles.

So what steps can you take to improve your chances of success in a relationship? There are two sets of skills you can develop as bases for survival strategies. The first is aimed at enhancing feelings of love.

Communication: Many partners find that their love can grow only if they can communicate honestly and openly. Chapter Three sets out the basics of how to communicate.

Expression of love through words and deeds: Many couples have found that they can learn ways of expressing love and affection that greatly enhance their satisfaction with their relationship.

Sexual expression: Satisfactory sexual relations are an important part of a relationship. Sexual awareness and a willingness to explore new modes of sexual expression can help a couple survive.

However, it is seldom enough for couples to develop strategies to build their love; they also need strategies that will prevent daily frustrations and conflicts from destroying their relationship. The second set of survival skills can be very valuable in helping couples deal with the conflicts and problems that arise in a long-term relationship. They include problem-solving, negotiation, fair fighting, effective division of labor and a constructive approach to independence, particularly sexual independence. These skills are described beginning in Chapter Six.

3

Effective Communication: Laying the Foundations

Jim, twenty-nine, the manager of a shoe department in a large retail store, and Betty, twenty-eight, a research assistant at a university, attended one of our couple-survival courses not because of any particular crisis in their relationship, but because each had become bored with the other. Although they had not experienced any major sexual difficulties, sexual contact between them had gradually declined to once a month; clearly neither of them was nearly as satisfied with their sexual life as they had been during the first three years of their seven-year relationship. Originally, they had talked of starting a family by the time each reached thirty, but neither had broached the subject of Betty going off the pill. Both were concerned that if something did not enliven their relationship, they would follow the route taken by several of their siblings and friends: divorce. One result of the dissatisfaction they felt with their relationship was that during the previous two years Jim, with Betty's consent, had begun to have casual affairs with other women.

Like all couples who join our survival courses, the first step was to have Jim and Betty participate in a full couple checkup. This entailed an hour-long couple interview, brief meetings between the consultant and each partner alone, the completion of several questionnaires and the videotaping of a thirty-minute conversation between Jim and Betty. The checkup results showed that Jim and Betty would be excellent candidates for the course; their first task should be to learn how to communicate more effectively. Three two-and-a-half-hour meetings later, Jim and Betty, much to their surprise and satisfaction, had significantly improved their communication skills.

Most couples find that they can best learn ways to improve their communication strategies by contrasting effective communication skills with ineffective ones. Let us see how Jim and Betty interacted during the preliminary couple checkup and how much more effectively they were able to communicate after survival-skills training.

Examples of Ineffective Communication

During the couple checkup Jim and Betty were asked to discuss a recent positive experience they had shared. Here's an extract from their discussion:

JIM: Okay, what shall we talk about?

BETTY *(looking tense)*: Gee, I don't know. What about that movie we saw last night?

JIM *(appearing visibly relieved that they had something to discuss)*: Good idea. You go first.

BETTY: Well, I liked the film, but you didn't seem to.

JIM *(in a low voice, looking away from Betty)*: I did fall asleep during the middle, but I liked the ending.

After each had looked at the other for about thirty seconds, the interviewer suggested they discuss another positive event, say a recent trip. Again they discussed the topic curtly and ineffectively. The interviewer then asked them to take turns giving the other support over a recent frustrating or stressful event at work.

JIM *(warming to the task)*: Would you like to start?

BETTY: Sure.

JIM: Well, since the new owner bought the store I feel under more pressure than ever.

BETTY *(looking at him while he speaks, but expressionless and motionless)*: You could always look for another job. *(trying to be helpful)*

JIM *(getting visibly uptight)*: Not with 15 per cent unemployment I couldn't!

After another thirty seconds of silence, the interviewer suggested they discuss a stressful situation Betty had recently experienced.

BETTY *(with more life in her voice)*: I love my job in the lab, but I'm always worried that you will resent the long hours I work, especially when I'm not home to make your supper.

JIM *(unconvincingly)*: I thought you didn't have any choice but to work those hours. If that's what you have to do to keep your job, why don't you talk to your boss about it?

BETTY *(sounding apologetic)*: Well, he's peculiar. He never notices the long hours I have to work to get anything done, but he does give me a lot of praise for my work.

JIM *(irritably)*: Well, you know best about your job. I don't know a thing about chemistry.

After a long silence the interviewer asked the partners to discuss several other topics.

Later, when asked as part of the couple checkup how they found the discussion sessions, both partners said they felt uncomfortable at first but had soon overcome their unease. Both acknowledged that with a few exceptions their conversation was much like the dialogue they had at home. When asked how they felt about the quality of their exchanges, they responded this way:

JIM *(looking depressed)*: When we first got married, we never ran out of things to talk about. But now it seems there is nothing new to say. Betty knows what I think and I know what she thinks. We both ran into life's problems, but how can we help each other? What good is there in talking about our worries?

BETTY *(looking discouraged)*: Well, I wish we could talk more. Many times after supper the TV is on, or when we're driving to work the radio is blaring, and we never get to talk at all. Certainly, we say very little to each other, but I don't agree with Jim that we know each other too well. At times I feel we talk more to strangers or to colleagues at work than we do to each other.

JIM *(getting upset)*: So maybe we are talking less, but isn't that the case with all couples who have been together for seven years?

Do conversations like these sound familiar to you? Jim and Betty's style of communicating resembles that of a large percentage of couples who have participated in our couple checkups. Did you spot some of the ineffective communication strategies each partner adopted? What effect do you think these might have on their relationship in the long run?

Now let's take a look at how they interacted after working on their communication strategies.

Examples of Effective Communication

The effective communication strategy employed in the dialogue below appears in italics after the message.

BETTY: I've noticed that we have not been getting out of the house much on weekends. *(She uses "I." She keeps her intervention short. She chooses a topic that is of importance to her.)*

JIM: So you figure we're not getting out as much as we used to. *(He summarizes what Betty said. In this way she knows he's listening. At the same time, he makes sure he understands her message.)* How do you feel about that? *(He asks Betty a question to encourage her to talk more.)*

BETTY: Well, I feel we would have more fun together if we shared new experiences. *(She expresses her opinion. She keeps her statement brief.)* What do you think? *(She encourages Jim to share his point of view with her.)*

JIM: Well, sometimes I do feel bored at home, but on the whole I really like it there. Our house is finally the way we want it. I have my workroom. I can hear you humming upstairs. I guess I simply don't feel as much need to go out as you do. *(He uses "I." He expresses his feelings. He acknowledges that they have different needs, but he does not criticize Betty's for being different than his.)*

BETTY: You feel happy at home and figure that we're different because I like to go out more. Is that right? *(She summarizes his response and seeks to confirm that she's understood him correctly.)*

JIM: Mmm. *(He indicates that she's right but does not speak, so as to encourage her to give her own view.)*

BETTY: Well, I do enjoy our nice relaxed times at home, but on the few occasions when we've made enough effort to go out and do something on the town, we've both ended up really enjoying ourselves. When I come home after a movie or a party I appreciate you and our home more than if we stay in all weekend. *(She uses "I." She keeps her message short. She manages to describe her ideal weekend without criticizing Jim for being more of a homebody. She does not demand that they come to an agreement on their differences.)*

If you return to the discussions Betty and Jim had prior to their communication-skills training and contrast these with the above conversation, you will appreciate the headway the couple has made. At the same time, you will be able to distinguish clearly between effective and ineffective styles of communicating.

Couples like Jim and Betty, who are mildly distressed, or those who are hostile, cite lack of communication as the most frequent source of discord. Communication means different things to different people; but in general, partners hope that they will be listened to, understood, supported and respected. Many hope that by keeping lines of communication open they will be better able to share life's joys and sorrows. Others believe that by talking together they can remain close to their partner. All these aspirations are attainable if the two partners learn the two sets of communication skills outlined below.

It Takes Two to Communicate: A Speaker and A Listener

If they are to communicate effectively, partners must be able to assume the two roles of speaker and listener. We all know couples who are good at one role but not at the other, couples who, for example, are both good talkers but poor listeners. These partners tend to talk loudly, to interrupt frequently and to complain of feeling alone and misunderstood. Couples like Jim and Betty seldom talk to each other and rarely share opinions or feelings. These partners are usually good listeners but generally only practise this skill outside their relationship. Their partnership is often marked by long silences and boredom, which at times hide feelings of tension, anger and depression. Other couples have complementary communication skills: one is a good listener, the other a good speaker; but neither is expert at both skills. These partners can be relatively stable and satisfied with their relationship, but there is a danger that the good speaker will become bored with the good listener, while the good listener may feel short-changed or misunderstood.

To master both skills, partners must become accustomed to assuming both roles in a conversation. One advantage to this exercise is that while you're working hard to be a good listener you know that your role will soon change to that of the speaker, so you will not become overly impatient with the conversation.

Here are six speaker strategies that can help improve dialogue between intimate partners. These are followed by four rules that can upgrade your listening skills.

Six Speaker Strategies for Effective Expression in an Intimate Relationship

1. Find a topic you can share.
2. Take responsibility for what you say by using the pronoun "I."
3. Use short messages.

4. Encourage your partner to listen by asking him/her questions.
5. Praise your partner for her/his efforts to understand you.
6. When discussing points of disagreement, aim for understanding, not agreement.

Strategy 1: Find a topic you can share. Many couples who have been together for several years claim they have nothing to talk about. When there is an opportunity to talk, some individuals, like Betty, feel at a genuine loss for words. Betty confessed: "I seldom have anything to say that will interest Jim." Couples have found the following list useful in choosing topics of mutual interest.

Leisure: films and television programs you enjoy; musical compositions and books you treasure; journeys you have made together; hobbies you both pursue.

Sports: games you participate in together or separately; spectator sports; the sporting pursuits of your children.

Projects for the future: plans for building a new home; for traveling; for changing careers.

Children: their similarities and differences; the way they play; the way they learn.

Work inside the home: tasks you enjoy and dislike; improvements that have to be made; projects already completed.

Work outside the home: difficult decisions to be made at the office; funny experiences with co-workers; unexpected events.

"Positive" feelings: pleasurable emotions – satisfaction, pride, sexual desire, sensual delight, trust, attraction, hope, challenge and ambition – can be rewarding for both of you if you share them.

"Negative" feelings: some painful emotions – anxiety, confusion, stress, discouragement, fear of illness, loneliness, dependence, sexual frustration, anger and inadequacy – if shared effectively, can draw partners closer together.

Family background and past: your childhood memories; your feelings for parents and siblings; your previous relationships.

Friendships: the pleasures and frustrations of your current friendships.

Politics and the community: your beliefs; your shared readings of issues in the news; your active participation in political and social events.

Spiritual values: the beliefs that guide your conscience.

Education: the courses you are taking or plan to take, and why they interest you.

Stragegy 2. Take responsibility for what you say by using the pronoun "I." This may sound like a simplistic suggestion, but you would be surprised at the difference it can make to a conversation.

In this dialogue, Jim and Betty attempt to give each other compliments:

JIM: Let's see. Your hair is luxuriously long and shiny, and your eyes sparkle.

BETTY: Thank you. Men of your generation are much better than younger men at telling a woman what they like about her.

Although they were asked to express their own feelings, neither did so clearly. Jim opens with "us" ("Let's") instead of "I." He expresses his appreciation of Betty's hair and eyes, but the compliments would have been far more effective if he had simply said: "I like your hair and eyes." Jim's approach keeps Betty unclear about how he really feels. It also keeps her at arm's length. Betty is just as ineffective. She refers to men in general instead of to Jim. By failing to respond to his compliment with "I," she keeps Jim at arm's length and in the dark about her true feelings.

Once the couple had practised using "I' they were able to reword their compliments:

JIM: I'm excited by your shiny hair and sparkly eyes.

BETTY: I love it when you flatter me. You can still give me goose-bumps.

Using the word "I" increases closeness between partners and facilitates better understanding of feelings. It also enables both individuals to take a legitimate place in the relationship.

Often when partners replace "I" by the pronouns "we" or "it" they are hiding their true emotions, both from themselves and from their spouse. For example, Jim and Betty attempted to express their feelings about their frustrating sexual relationship as follows:

BETTY: Isn't it interesting how couples who have been married for several years have sex less often.

JIM: Maybe they would like to indulge more, but too many obstacles like kids, work and fatigue stand in the way.

Betty has generalized her feelings by speaking of "couples." Similarly, Jim has used "they." The impact is to keep each other at bay. They have avoided expressing emotions that could have led both partners to feel perhaps a little anxious at first but ultimately closer together. After practice with "I" in the survival sessions, Betty was able to say: "I am worried that we make love so seldom. I'm afraid it means I don't excite you anymore, and that you'll find another woman to replace me, if you haven't done so already." Jim was able to admit: "I'm afraid I must be getting older because I get the urge to make love less often."

By using the first-person pronoun, the responsibility for identifying and owning up to emotions falls squarely on each individual's shoulders. If two partners do not take turns attempting to identify and express their feelings, much of the interaction between them will be difficult to comprehend and even more difficult to control. One of the first steps to improving sexual relations (discussed in Chapter Six) is to take responsibility for identifying what activities you like and dislike in bed. This is only possible if each partner can say "I feel" instead of "you feel," "we feel" or "couples feel."

By not using "I" in their discussions, Jim and Betty avoided feeling that they differed from each other. Since their early courtship days, both had been struck by how similar they were in background, education, preferences and preoccupations. Both had believed that only very similar people could survive in an intimate relationship. They feared that if they should develop different interests and feelings, such changes would signify the beginning of the end of their partnership. As we will see in Chapter Eight, differences between intimates are not only inevitable, they are essential for maintaining the quality and intensity of a relationship.

By using "I," partners can no longer pretend that differences between them do not exist: they cannot fail to notice that "I" is not synonymous with "we." Moreover, such recognition is not only desirable but is also beneficial to all intimate relationships.

Strategy 3: Use short messages. Fifty per cent of the responsibility for a good conversation rests on the shoulders of the listener. Using nods, questions and summaries, he/she encourages the speaker to express opinions and feelings openly. In turn, the speaker can make life easier for the listener by not monopolizing the conversation with more than two or three statements at a time. Couples commonly find discussions more lively if each interjects her/his point of view every minute or so. Partners who are not used to revealing their thoughts or who have seldom had the attentive ear of their partner or who have an opinion that they eagerly want their partner to accept can make the mistake of speaking too long, monopolizing the conversation for what can seem to be an interminable time.

The dangers of such behavior are numerous.

(a) If a partner cannot get a word in edgewise, he/she may lose interest in the conversation.

(b) If one partner monopolizes the role of speaker, it is only to be expected that the other will do likewise when he/she gets to speak.

(c) If one partner does not allow the other to exercise the listening skills of summarizing, questioning and clarifying, the speaker will not know whether he/she has understood. As a result, a long speech will not have the desired effect: the speaker will not feel understood and the listener will not feel the satisfaction of having actively listened.

Strategy 4: Encourage your partner to listen by asking him/her questions. The effective speaker need not be preoccupied with the listener's ability to understand; the main responsibility for understanding lies with the listener. Nevertheless, the speaker can make the listener's role much easier and hold her/his attention by occasionally asking such questions as: "Do you understand what I mean?" or "How do you feel?" or "What do you think?"

Strategy 5: Praise your partner for her/his efforts to understand you. Many partners fall into the trap of assuming that if their partner loves them, then he/she is obliged to listen and understand. Most, however, listen not out of duty but because they feel their partner will appreciate their efforts to do so. Responses such as: "Thanks for trying to understand" or "Thank you for helping me get that problem off my chest" or "I enjoyed talking" can go a long way to encourage the listener to repeat his/her efforts.

During their third communication-skills session, Betty and Jim had the following discussion, which illustrates their command of the first five strategies:

JIM: This afternoon the new boss walked through my department four times. I never saw my old boss more than once a month. *(He uses "I" and chooses a topic they can share.)*

BETTY: How did his visits make you feel? *(She asks a clear, open-ended question.)*

JIM: I felt I was under a spotlight, that I had a detective following me. I really wanted to tell him to stop putting the pressure on. (pause) What do you think I should do? *(He questions the listener and thereby keeps her involved in the conversation.)*

After pinpointing the various options open to Jim, they pursued the issue a little farther and then commented upon the improvements they'd made in communicating.

JIM: It does feel good to get the subject off my chest. I have to admit, though, that I don't know the new boss well enough yet. So far he has not criticized me in any way, and maybe he means well. I would be foolish to show my irritation with him. It is, after all, his store. Now that we've talked about the situation, I feel much less anxious about it. You really know how to get me talking, Betty. *(He praises her for having been a good listener.)*

BETTY *(smiling and obviously pleased with the progress they've made)*: Well, I am glad you've told me about the problem. Now I understand why you come home in a lousy mood sometimes. You know, you're just as good at encouraging me to open up. Last night, for example, in the car on the way home from the office, you helped me talk about the confrontation I had with one of my co-workers. I appreciated that. *(She praises him for having been a good listener.)*

Strategy 6: When discussing points of disagreement, aim first for understanding, not agreement. Many couples, especially those who fight often, tend to want "to win." If a speaker suspects that her/his partner does not agree with the argument, the speaker will persist in trying to convince her/his mate to change points of view. The problem is that the speaker is essentially saying to his/her partner, "admit you're wrong" or "change your attitude." The listener, feeling antagonized, will not remain long in his/her role. If a couple's goal is to increase understanding and sharing through effective communication, the speaker must first ensure that the listener understands what the speaker thinks and feels. Partners often confuse understanding of a point of view with agreement.

Jim and Betty found strategy six one of the most difficult to master, but they recognized that it was the one that most helped them improve their ability to communicate. One discussion early in the communication-skills training sounded like this:

BETTY: We would have more fun together if we got out of the house more on weekends. *(She has not used "I." She has not expressed her feelings.)*

JIM: No, we couldn't be happier. Our weekends are perfect. *(He has not used "I." He has not tried to understand her point of view.)*

BETTY: You're not listening to what I'm saying.

Clearly, both might have approached this subject differently and more effectively. If each partner had used "I," the conversation would have been far less confusing and tense. Because Betty brought up a subject that she knew had caused many disagreements in the past, Jim's first reaction was to disagree with her rather than to try to understand her point of view, by rushing in to push his own opinion. After practising strategy six, Betty and Jim had a second discussion on the same subject:

BETTY: I feel I would have more fun on weekends if we got out of the house more often. *(She uses "I" and only expresses her own feelings, without suggesting what Jim should feel.)*

JIM *(adopting an attentive tone and body posture)*: So, you figure you would have more fun if we got out more often. *(He tries to understand what she was saying without pushing his own view first.)*

BETTY: Mmm. What do you think? *(She, feeling understood, is now more interested in discovering his feelings.)*

JIM: Well, I think we are different. I'm more of a homebody. But the last time we went to a movie and had that Chinese meal I certainly had fun. *(He succeeds in admitting they are different, but that when they follow her preference he can have fun, too.)*

How to Improve Your Listening Skills

Many partners believe they are excellent listeners. Our research shows, however, that few actually are. One of the best ways to find out whether you listen effectively to your partner is to tape-record one of your conversations. When you play it back, pay attention only to the way in which you listen. Then judge yourself a good, mediocre or poor listener using these four rules for effective listening:

1. Listen with your body and voice.
2. Encourage the speaker to talk.
3. Summarize your partner's message to be sure you understand it and to show that you are listening.

4. When in doubt about your partner's message, ask questions.

Once you have studied and practised with your partner the rules for effective listening that follow, it will be useful to test your listening skills again.

There has been more intensive research on the skills required of the effective listener than on most other areas of human psychology. Most couples find that it is not as difficult to learn straightforward listening strategies as it is to remember to doff the speaker's hat for the listener's. Couples who frequently take turns to listen actively to each other enjoy a great degree of closeness and trust.

Strategy 1: Listen with your body and voice. When we listen to our partner our words may say one thing and our bodies another. For example, while our partner is speaking we may say, "Tell me more," or "That's interesting," but are we also listening with our body? Did we yawn? Did we continue to read the newspaper? Did we have a glazed look in our eyes? The "tell me more" part of our message is its verbal content, but of equal importance is the nonverbal component, body language.

Couples who want to improve their listening skills should be aware of four kinds of body language: eye contact, facial expression, body action and body position. Take a look at how you listen to your spouse, your children, your friends and colleagues. Then examine the chart that presents nonverbal messages that tell your partner you are not listening, even though you say you are.

Body Position or Action

Nonverbal channel	"I'm listening"	"I'm not listening"	Your "not-listening" message
Eyes	On speaker	Not on speaker, or rarely on speaker	"I don't care" "You make me nervous"

(continued on next page)

(continued)

Face	Open, attentive expression	Scowl	"I disagree"
		Yawn	"You bore me"
Body action	Nodding of head	None	"I don't follow you"
		Shaking of head	"I disagree"
		Reading of newspaper	"You bore me" "I'm not listening
		Watching the children	"They're more important"
Body position	Straight to-ward speaker	Turned away from speaker	"I'm not listening"

Research[2] has found that the intended messages between highly distressed partners are often misinterpreted. One frequent cause for this is the disparity between verbal and nonverbal expression.

Examine this interaction between many partners: One partner (the speaker) comes home from work, and the other partner (the listener) asks: "How was your day?" The speaker responds: "Rough." The listening partner then says, "Tell me all about it," but continues to do what he/she was doing before the speaker arrived: fixing supper, reading the newspaper or repairing the automobile.

If a partner sends one message ("I'm not listening") with his/her body and another ("I am listening") with words, the speaker feels confusion, anger and a lack of motivation to continue speaking.

Strategy 2: Encourage the speaker to talk. Simple words of encouragement like "I see," "go on," "tell me more" can make a surprising difference to how much the speaker will be willing to reveal.

Strategy 3: Summarize your partner's message to be sure you understand it and to show that you are listening. One of the most demanding and most powerful tools of the good listener is to reflect to your partner the essence of what he/she is saying. This dialogue between Betty and Jim took place after they had practised this listening skill:

JIM: So what subject shall we discuss?

BETTY: How about sex?

JIM: Okay, you start.

BETTY: Well, I've noticed we make love less often now.

JIM: You've noticed we don't have sex as often as before.

BETTY: But I think we love each other as much as ever.

JIM: Mmm. You think we're still in love, but we don't make love as often as in the beginning of our relationship.

Jim's tactic was to repeat to Betty her own words or very similar ones. As a result, Jim reported: "I felt I didn't want to miss anything Betty said, so I hung on her every word." Betty reacted this way: "I felt listened to and understood as I rarely have before. I felt I was in the hot seat, and it made me a little shy, but I felt we could really go somewhere with our discussion. It especially encouraged me to open up, to really say what was on my mind."

Betty and Jim identified four advantages to the exercise: it forces the listener to remain alert; it enables the speaker to feel understood; it helps avoid misunderstanding between partners; and it encourages the speaker to explore her/his own feelings, in order to come to better self-understanding.

When it was Jim's turn to disclose his feelings on the same topic, the dialogue went as follows:

JIM: You know it was only when you were speaking that I realized I also was worried about the fact we aren't making love so often. But I'm not quite sure why it worries me.

BETTY: So you're also concerned about our love-making but you're not sure why.

JIM: I was worried that you would think I loved you less, but that's not true.

BETTY: So you feel you still love me, but you were worried I didn't know it.

Betty and Jim have learned to summarize; and, as the extract above shows, it has already helped them improve the openness of their communication.

Strategy 4: When in doubt as to your partner's message, ask questions. Often when we are having a conversation with our partner he/she will say something that we do not fully understand. We may be tempted just to let our partner continue or we may tell our partner what we thought he/she meant. Another simple and effective skill the listener can employ is to ask questions.

There are many types of questions. The listening partner should choose a question that will help the speaker continue her/his own self-exploration. Closed questions, "why" questions and questions that change the subject should be avoided because they reflect only what the listener wants to hear. Below are examples of the kinds of questions that might be posed by effective and ineffective listeners on the subject Jim and Betty were discussing:

Effective listener	*Ineffective listener*
Do you want to tell me more about how you feel about our sex life? *(an open question)*	So you think our sexual relationship is in trouble? *(a closed question)*
Do you mean you still feel loving toward me even though we don't make love as often as before? *(a question to verify the speaker's meaning)*	I am surprised to hear you say you still love me even though we make love so rarely. *(a statement from the listener, not a question to the speaker)*
You seem to be concerned that we don't make love more often. Do you want to talk about it? *(a·reflective statement and a question that encourages talk)*	So you're worried about our sex life, and that our marriage is on the rocks? *(a closed question and one that changes the subject)*

58

Some couples find this exercise difficult:

"I'll feel phony if I ask in those ways, and my partner will think I'm ridiculous."

Any new behavior or speech pattern feels awkward at first. With practice, though, you'll soon feel more at ease. Most people in the speaker role enjoy it when their partner actively listens to them. It feels good to be listened to.

"It will take too much time and energy to change my ways."

At first it takes a lot of energy to change mental and verbal habits, especially if you've been a lazy listener. I'm not suggesting you actively listen to each other all day – that could drive both of you to exhaustion. However, if you want to derive real benefits from communicating with your partner, and if you really want to have solid, constructive discussions, then the four listening strategies we have described will help you along the way.

Obstacles to Improving Communication Skills

Now that you have studied the six strategies for improving your ability to speak and the four strategies for becoming a better listener, you may wish to start work on improving your own communication skills. First, however, you should be aware of three obstacles that must be overcome:

1. Misconceptions that can interfere with sending effective messages between intimate partners.
2. Misconceptions that can prevent effective listening between partners.
3. Expecting communication skills to solve all the problems in a relationship.

1. Misconceptions about effective speaking. Some of the more frequent, inhibiting misconceptions are summarized in the table below. For each negative idea that inhibits effective use of the speaker strategies, there is a positive antidote to encourage use of the strategy.

Misconceptions that inhibit effective speaking	Beliefs that encourage effective speaking
My partner knows me so well that talking about my inner thoughts or feelings would be a waste of time.	If I do not regularly communicate my thoughts and feelings to my partner, we will gradually become strangers.
Why should I talk about my inner feelings? Words change nothing.	If we both follow effective speaking and listening rules we will understand each other and feel closer.
If I reveal too much about my feelings, my partner will judge, criticize or punish me. If I say what's on my mind, my partner will surely get angry.	If we allow enough time, and are honest but careful about what we say, we should be able to discuss most topics successfully. This will especially be true if we learn problem-solving and fair-fighting techniques.
Only weak people talk about their feelings.	Talking honestly about my feelings will take more courage than silence, but the rewards I reap through opening up to my partner are well worth the risks I must take.
If my partner cared more, he/she would know how I feel without me having to spell it out.	Nobody can read minds. If I want my partner to know what's on my mind I must speak.

Let us explore each of the misconceptions we have outlined.

"My partner knows me so well that talking about my inner thoughts or feelings would be a waste of time." Partners who

have lived together for a long time often tend to talk about the same things, out of habit. Yet there are many topics of interest they can share. When one partner invests the time and energy to disclose thoughts or feelings, the other needs to concentrate on employing effective listening strategies to ensure that the speaker isn't forced to conclude that talking is a waste of time because her/his partner is not interested in what he/she has to say.

"Why should I talk about my inner feelings? Words change nothing." This attitude is seen in couples who have never communicated too successfully and have lost touch with each other's thoughts. One of the most frequent causes is related to the conversational strategies that partners in a relationship adopt as speaker and listener and will influence their opinions on the effectiveness of words. Let's return to Jim and Betty's first conversation in this chapter; you will recall it was about the film they saw together. (See p. 43). The way they spoke would reinforce the opinion that talking isn't worth the trouble.

Betty told Jim that she had liked the film without telling him why; she then assumed that he hadn't liked the movie without asking. By short-circuiting the conversation, Betty forfeited the benefits of both speaking and listening. Similarly, Jim offered very little and didn't encourage Betty to talk about her impressions.

Jim and Betty learned simply to listen, without giving advice, and each discovered how good it felt to talk and be understood by someone else. Both felt that their conversations took on new significance because they could now understand each other.

"If I reveal too much about my feelings, my partner will judge, criticize or punish me." Couples who are constantly at each other's throats or on the verge of separation are unlikely to share their deepest feelings successfully. Such "warring" couples would be best advised either to learn how to fight fairly or to separate constructively.

However, couples who argue frequently but who are not in a state of war can profit enormously from the time spent quietly talking and listening. Admittedly, if every time one partner speaks the other criticizes, little constructive communication is possible. Couples need to begin constructive discussions during peaceful moments, and each partner should adopt the attitude: "I'll give you a chance to talk without criticizing if you will do the same for me." A couple can work together in this way only as long as both partners follow the constructive-speaking and active-listening strategies.

"If I say what's on my mind, my partner will surely get angry." This misconception resembles the previous one, with one important difference: here the speaker is afraid the listener will become not only critical but angry, and that he/she will retaliate with words and actions. Some partners are justified in not wanting to risk the consequences of self-disclosure and should probably leave some subjects untouched until certain aspects of their relationship improve. But for many intimates this is merely an excuse.

It is the responsibility of the speaker to learn how to talk about frustrating feelings without blaming the listener. Speaker Strategy Six ("When discussing points of disagreement, aim for understanding, not agreement.") can be a valuable aid here. Timing is also crucial: the speaker must choose the right moment to talk about touchy subjects. An overly cautious couple will learn that the risks taken in self-disclosure and active listening are usually well worth the increased trust, understanding and intimacy that result.

Both Betty and Jim were surprised to learn that subjects they were sure would infuriate the other invoked responses as diverse as relief, curiosity and laughter when approached slowly and carefully.

"Only weak people talk about their feelings." As children, we may have been heavily indoctrinated with such myths as: "Only sissies cry," "Only girls are afraid of the dark," "Only weaklings get tired" and so on. Many of us still suffer the inhibiting effects of such socialization. Yet people who keep their feelings bottled up risk ulcers, heart problems and so on. They are also more inclined to experience loneliness and to re-

main outside the emotional life of the family. It takes more courage to talk honestly and openly about our positive and negative feelings than it does to keep them inside. A partner who refuses to open up will miss out on the rich experience of knowing that someone else cares and understands her/his feelings.

"If my partner cared more, he/she would know how I feel without me having to spell it out." This position is at times somewhat justified. However, in most intimate relationships, a lack of open communication is not the fault of one partner alone. Usually both are working with certain misconceptions and significant deficiencies in speaking and listening skills.

"If you cared you could read my mind." This presumption is unreasonable and unworkable. A partner who takes this stance is placing an impossible demand on her/his relationship. Try these constructive antidotes: "If I love you I won't try to read your mind, I'll ask you what you feel" and "If I love you I will tell you what's on my mind so you won't have to guess."

2. Misconceptions that can prevent effective listening between partners. Some couples entertain ideas that prevent them from learning or practising effective listening strategies. Four typical misconceptions are listed in the table below. Each is paired with a constructive antidote.

Suppositions that block effective listening	Antidotes that help listening
Listening won't be enough.	Often "just listening" makes all the difference.
If I listen and show that I understand, my partner will think I agree with everything he/she is saying.	I can show I understand without agreeing.
Why should I listen when my partner won't listen to me?	If we take turns listening, we can improve communication between us.

(continued on next page)

I'm too angry to listen.	When I'm angry, listening can help me understand and can help us feel closer. An effective listening session may initiate a problem-solving session that will help resolve our differences.

"Listening won't be enough." Many people feel that they should do something more. If your partner is describing a painful experience, you might feel compelled to offer sympathy or a suggestion. Stop yourself: continue to listen attentively. Often the speaker will need understanding more than she/he needs a solution.

Some people have difficulty "just listening" while their partner describes satisfaction, appreciation or admiration. The listener may feel embarrassed or want to return the appreciation by demonstrating affection with a hug or caress. Remember, however, that listening is often the best way to show that you care.

Betty and Jim's second conversation, about Betty's work (see page 44), should prompt a rewarding discussion between partners, if they have the skills and the right attitude to keep the conversation going.

However, instead of summarizing what Betty had said, using the listener's skills of reflection, clarification and encouragement, Jim jumped in with a suggestion for a solution. When asked about this he protested, "I felt that if I didn't help Betty find a solution to her problem then I would be letting her down."

Betty tended to follow the same type of pattern, with the result that neither would spend much time talking about troublesome feelings: either the speaker would cut the conversation short if a solution didn't spring to mind or the listener would interrupt with a suggestion.

"If I listen and show that I understand, my partner will think I agree with everything he/she is saying." Many partners

confuse understanding with agreement. Conrad and Susan are a couple who have daily arguments that don't resolve anything. They found that even when they began by respecting the communication rules, conversations often turned into fights over differences of opinion. Conrad would protest: "How can you expect me to listen to her if I don't agree?" Yet many of their important differences of opinion could be resolved only when each actively listened to the other's opinion without interrupting.

"Why should I listen when my partner won't listen to me?" Susan and Conrad often played this "you-go-first" game, so their discussions frequently came to a standstill with neither listening to the other. To avoid an impasse, partners should use their listening responses even if they sense that their partner has not listened attentively.

"I'm too angry to listen." Couples who fight frequently often allow their listening skills to degenerate. By being "too angry to listen," they are refusing to dissipate their anger. Admittedly, in certain volatile situations it is better to declare a moratorium on communication until both partners cool off. (See Chapter Nine.) However, many couples have learned that if both partners exercise some self-control and respect the speaking and listening rules, they can listen even though they feel somewhat angry. By listening in spite of their anger, they begin to understand why their partner acted in a way that made them angry.

3. Expecting communication skills to solve all problems in a relationship. Some approaches to couple enrichment place almost exclusive emphasis on communication skills. However, we believe that couples who have mastered communication skills should go on to learn strategies that will help them to express their emotions, to solve problems and to fight. Survival skills in addition to effective communication are needed to deal with the variety of situations that intimate partners face.

Most couples who are satisfied with their relationship know that their success is due in part to a developed sense of timing:

knowing when to get angry, when to listen, when to offer support, when to solve problems, when to give each other breathing space and when to make love. If both partners remember that most situations can be approached in several ways, then, once they have communicated their honest impressions of the circumstances at hand, they can ask, "What should we do now?" They may decide that communication is enough, or they may go on to solve problems, have a fight or make love.

How to Practise Communication Skills

If you and your partner have decided to make a concerted effort to develop these communications-survival strategies, these guidelines will prove invaluable when practising at home. While each guideline applies to communication skills, all eight are also important to practising all survival strategies.

One: Decide when and for how long you will practise. Some couples who are keen to improve their communication skills attempt to use the suggested strategies every moment they are together. Don't be too ambitious; either or both of you may become bored or frustrated. Start with several practice sessions totalling thirty minutes a week. Carefully plan suitable times for your sessions. This "schedule" for practice sessions could be negotiated each week, written down and posted in an obvious place as a reminder.

During the first few weeks of practice it is usually better to be alone, so choose a time when children, family, friends or colleagues will leave you undisturbed.

Two: Begin with easy, non-sensitive topics. Don't try to move too fast. Your changes of improvement may be endangered when skills that you have only partially mastered won't stand the test of demanding issues. Begin practising your listening skills in conversations about pleasurable events. Only when you have mastered these strategies and other essential communication techniques should you venture into more difficult areas.

To choose nonthreatening topics for your first practice sessions, each partner might make a list of five subjects. If you are at a loss for ideas, consult Speaker Strategy 1 ("Find a topic you can share" – see p. 48). Exchange lists and circle those subjects both agree will not be too sensitive.

Remember that the practice sessions are not designed to give you a chance to talk about something that has been on your mind for years, but to help you learn communication skills. You will need to concentrate both on speaking and on listening, so choose topics that are not so engrossing that they distract you from concentrating.

Three: Remember the six Speaker Strategies (see p. 47) and four Listener Rules (see p. 54). Treat the practice sessions as a "back-to-school" exercise. You will find it helpful to memorize the ten strategies and rules so you will have them at your fingertips during a discussion. List the six Speaker Strategies and four Listener Rules to jog your memory.

Four: Compare your interpretation of the strategies and rules. Don't be surprised if your partner's reading of any of the communication strategies is different from your own. Avoid any potential confusion by comparing your interpretations.

Five: Master one listener skill and one speaker skill at a time. Look over the lists of Speaker Strategies and Listening Rules and pick the one you feel to be the simplest of each. Begin with these two skills. Feel free to start by practising skills that you feel you have already mastered. You will find that communication skills will come more easily to you if you are confident in your abilities from the start.

Self-monitoring for
Couple Communication Skills

Place an x beside skill practised today		How often used successfully during discussion?
	Six Speaker Rules	
_____	1. Find a topic you can share.	_____
_____	2. Take responsibility for what you say by using the pronoun "I."	_____
_____	3. Use short messages.	_____
_____	4. Encourage your partner to listen by asking him/her questions.	_____
_____	5. Praise your partner for her/his efforts to understand you.	_____
_____	6. When discussing points of disagreement, aim first for understanding, not agreement.	_____

Place an x beside skill practised today		How often used successfully during discussion?
	Four Listener Rules	
_____	1. Listen with your body and voice.	_____
_____	2. Encourage the speaker to talk.	_____
_____	3. Summarize your partner's message to be sure you understand it and to show that you are listening.	_____
_____	4. When in doubt about your partner's message, ask questions.	_____

Six: Combine short practice discussions with frequent "self-feedback." The two most important components of the self-change program are practice and feedback. Do your best to follow the speaker and listener strategies you have chosen to work with. Several short practice sessions are better than one long session. The ideal length of a session at the beginning of a self-help program is two to three minutes. This is usually long enough for both partners to have played the roles of speaker and listener several times.

Stop and evaluate your own performance. Compile two self-monitoring forms (see p. 68) for each session to record your impressions of how successful you have been in following the listener rule and the speaker strategy chosen for that practice session. Self-feedback is usually more effective than feedback from your partner. It is safest, especially during your initial sessions, not to arouse anger, discouragement or competition by sharing your opinions of each other's success.

Seven: Use a tape recorder. Many partners find taping their practice sessions valuable. A taped version of your message will demonstrate how you sound to your partner and tell you how well your words and the tone of your voice have conveyed the message you intended.

Eight: Have fun and be patient. Do anything you can do to liven up your practice sessions. Tell jokes or choose an interesting setting – the bath, the beach, a park. Most couples find that months of practice are necessary before strategies have a lasting effect. Have one or two encouraging practice sessions per week for several months. If you cram four hours of practice into the first week and feel you have not progressed, you are likely to abandon your self-change program.

4

Strategies to Enhance Love

We must learn to be lovers. Many partners prefer to avoid knowing why or how they love, believing that the more mysterious a love, the more romantic. Building a love is a creative process, much more like painting a picture or playing a symphony than performing a mechanical function. Love will increase if both partners have or learn certain skills.

Lovers, like artists, accept that in order to reach their potential they must practise the rudimentary skills of their art. Most couples believe that the maintenance of love is basic to the survival of their relationship. Therefore, many are ready to sacrifice some of the mystery of their love for increased understanding and new skills that can enhance exchanges of affection.

These skills are infinite in number and complexity, but the following twelve steps are a good start:

Twelve Steps to Increase the Exchange of Love Between Intimate Partners

1. Take time alone to identify what each of you needs to feel loved.
2. Decide which of your desires are reasonable.
3. Accept that your needs and your partner's needs are not identical.
4. Take turns expressing and listening to each other's desires, attempting simply to understand, not to change them.
5. Identify which desires each is willing and able to satisfy.

6. Decide who will attempt to satisfy first.
7. Be consistent and fair.
8. Learn to express love and affection verbally.
9. Find new ways to express caring through actions.
10. Receive your partner's love and affection positively.
11. Constantly vary loving exchanges.
12. Overcome attitudes that may block new efforts to exchange love.

One: Take time alone to identify what each of you needs to feel loved. The first step requires that both partners grow to know themselves enough to understand what experiences are pleasurable to them. Concentrating on oneself is required. Many believe that only a match between two unselfish people will produce strong love. In fact, a delicate balance of the ability to give and the ability to receive is required. Many of us have experienced the frustration of trying unsuccessfully to satisfy a lover. Often this happens because the lover has failed to identify what would give satisfaction. Naturally, then, the first step to love enhancement requires that both partners know themselves and what they expect from the relationship.

Ask yourself: "What could my partner do or say that would make me feel good? What could we do or say together that would make me feel happy?" Some will find it easy to answer these questions; others will find it very difficult.

Rubin and Karen found these questions difficult at first. Rubin worked in his father's successful retail business and Karen was studying to be a computer programmer. They had one eight-year-old boy from Karen's previous marriage and a two-year-old boy from their own marriage. They were taking the survival course mainly as a preventive measure, "to improve our chances," Karen explained.

The following exchange between Rubin and Karen illustrates some of the problems involved in articulating needs.

RUBIN: So, I should try to write down what Karen could do to please me? It seems a bit surprising that we should have to do that now. We've been married for three years and were dating for a year before that. During the initial stages of our relationship, Karen seemed to know what I needed without my having to tell her.

Often partners find that during the early romantic phase of their relationship they both are working so hard to please the other that no asking is necessary. Then they enter a new era. When some of the romance has passed, if it isn't replaced with something more lasting, one or both partners might lose the sense that you are being satisfied.

RUBIN: Okay, I'll give it a try. But I must say I feel a bit weird writing this down.

KAREN: I'm willing to give it a try, although I do feel that if Rubin really cared he would know what I enjoy. (pause) Honestly, if he hasn't picked it up by now, it must be because he doesn't care.

Partners know something about each other's needs depending on how clearly they have communicated about love. They are often surprised, however, to learn just how intricate their fantasies are or what they could do together to make them happy.

KAREN: I've noticed within the past year we have started to fall into a rut. We've only been married three years and we already tend to follow the same routines week after week. At times, I flash on images of my mother and father, who just sat around saying nothing and doing nothing together after thirty years of marriage.

Many couples, if not most, experience this sooner or later in their relationship. Perhaps part of the boredom comes from too much reliance on the same pleasures week in and week out. The point of this "know-yourself" exercise is to discover a wider range of experiences that might satisfy you.

Rubin's reluctance to write down what he desires stemmed from his somewhat irrational question: "It wasn't necessary during our romance, why should it be now?" A fear of feeling embarrassed also blocked his effort to identify his wants.

Karen was asking, unreasonably, that Rubin read her mind. She was hesitant to pin down what she wanted from him because she felt he had already rejected requests that she thought had been clear. Both believed that what had satisfied them three years ago should satisfy them now. Neither seemed to recognize that time and habit had diminished the power of previously pleasurable events.

Try following the steps Rubin and Karen took. List the desires you would like your partner to fulfill. As you write, be aware of thoughts going through your head. Notice whether you hold some of the misconceptions that Rubin and Karen mentioned or others described earlier. Do you feel embarrassed? Are you concerned that all your requests will be rejected?

Two: Decide which of your own desires are reasonable. While you are alone, go through your list of wants. Mark an R beside those you feel are realistic wishes, an M beside those maybes that might be worth discussing with your partner and a U beside those you know are unrealistic. Conducting a reality test on your desires will help for several reasons. Once you have taken time to articulate your desires, you will realize that some are dreams that you have had for a long time; they may date back to your childhood and may be no longer realistic. You may want your partner to be always strong and never sick or old. Other wishes may be possible to realize, providing you don't ask that two or more be satisfied at the same time.

Rubin wrote, "I wish Karen were more available." At the same time, he also wished she would "develop more interests of her own." I emphasized that these two desires of Rubin's need not be incompatible. However, the couple needed to talk about these two wishes to be sure that Karen was not faced with a double bind. For if Karen developed more independent interests, Rubin risked seeing less of her; if she was more available for Rubin she would, of course, have less time for her independent interests. I suggested that Rubin place an M beside these two desires on his list and that both be topics for future discussion.

Many of our desires are probably legitimate and our partner might want to satisfy these wishes, but might not be able to at present. Karen wrote, "I wish Rubin would postpone his climax. Now he comes within ten seconds of entry." Rubin wanted very much to please Karen by delaying his ejaculation but, as is often the case, the harder he tried the less he succeeded. Karen and Rubin accepted that Karen's desire could be realized only if they both tried to change their sexual functioning. Nor was this a request that Karen could hope to have satisfied in the short term. We control some of our habits voluntarily; if we're willing to do so, we can easily change them. Other aspects of our functioning are intricately linked to our emotional makeup and our social skills and can only be changed through consistent long-term effort.

Three: Accept that your needs and your partner's needs are not identical. You must be prepared to discover that your desires and your partner's are not identical. You may want more sensual time together while your partner wants to take a trip with you. That you want different things does not necessarily mean that you will have a less fulfilling life together.

As we move to the next step; it is crucial to keep in mind that differences in loving are inevitable and not necessarily destructive. Communication about each partner's list of desires will be productive provided differences are seen as healthy rather than threatening to the relationship.

Four: Take turns expressing and listening to each other's desires, attempting simply to understand, not to change them. Remember the communications skills described in Chapter Three. The desires you have listed suggest ideal themes for practising self-disclosure and active listening. The purpose of this communication session is to take turns discussing each other's wishes. The objective is to understand, not to change. In this session, the listener should not feel compelled to accept or reject what the speaker is saying; nor should the speaker feel the need to justify her/his wishes.

Karen and Rubin had a thought-provoking discussion when they first attempted to exchange items from their lists.

RUBIN: Okay, who goes first – you or me?

KAREN: Doesn't matter, we'll go back and forth.

RUBIN: You'll probably get more chances to speak than to listen because my list is pretty short. Why don't you go first?

KAREN: Okay. I wish that you would make our romantic meal sometimes.

RUBIN: Now I'm supposed to be the active listener. Okay, you wish that I would be the chef sometimes for our romantic Friday-night dinners. How would that make you feel?

KAREN: More romantic, because I wouldn't just have spent an hour cooking.

RUBIN: You think you'd feel more romantic.

So far they have both found the disclosure and listening skills they had learned easy to apply. However, both found the next theme a little more difficult.

KAREN: Now it's your turn.

RUBIN: Okay. I feel a bit silly asking, but I wish you wouldn't be so cool to me when I come home from work.

KAREN: You want me to ask you what kind of day you had? *(defensively)* Why?

RUBIN *(accusingly)*: Yes. I work really heard and I'm not sure you even care.

KAREN *(attacking)*: I don't have to ask. When you've had a lousy day it's writtten all over your face.

Obviously Rubin had made a request that touched a nerve for both of them. How might they have avoided their discussion becoming an exchange of accusations? First, if Rubin had given examples of what he hoped Karen might do, the discussion could have been more precise and positive. If he had described how this change would have pleased him or the positive impact it could have on the relationship, it would have been easier for Karen to listen actively. Karen could have asked Rubin to clarify his request with: "How might this make you feel?" or "What might I do?" instead of "Why?" When these were pointed out to them they had the following discussion.

RUBIN *(calmly describing his desire and why he is making the request)*: When I come home from work it would make me feel good if you would start a conversation about my day.

KAREN *(loudly but not aggressively summarizing her interpretation of Rubin's request and then asking a good open question)*: You'd like me to discuss your day with you before supper. How do you think this would make you feel?

RUBIN *(still calmly explaining why he has made his request)*: Well, when I've had a bad day, if we talked a bit, I could get the tension off my chest. I feel I would be a better father, and a better husband, for the rest of the evening.

KAREN *(still calmly)*: Okay, you feel I can help you unwind after a hard day.

In this exchange Karen and Rubin followed the constructive communication rules well and returned to the issue after they had tackled the next step.

Five: Identify which desires each is willing and able to satisfy. Once you have listened to each other's list of desires, try to sort the requests that your partner has made into four types: (1) those requests that you are willing and able to satisfy now; (2) desires that you would like to satisfy but feel you don't yet know how; (3) desires that your are able to address but do not want to; and (4) desires that are unrealistic. Take turns conveying your impressions and classifying each request.

Couples who are accustomed to trying to please each other enjoy this exercise. You can now let your fantasies on ways of pleasing your partner run wild. Couples who seldom share affection through words or deeds can find this step very difficult.

Don't rush this step. You need to discuss your requests openly and calmly. All too often this type of communication is brushed aside until it can no longer be avoided. Then, little progress is made because the discussion has already degenerated into altercation.

Let us briefly look at the four classifications of requests.

1. *Those requests that you are willing and able to satisfy now.* Once you have listened to your partner's requests, identify those desires that you feel willing and able to satisfy. Saying you are interested in trying to satisfy a specific desire does not mean you will start tomorrow. Before making any specific plans, study all the recommended steps to increase your chances of success.

2. *Desires that you would like to satisfy but feel you don't yet know how.* As demonstrated by Karen and Rubin's discussion of their sexual problem, certain requests will require that one or both partners make certain changes in their behavior. Requests related to sensuality and sexuality, communication skills or exchange of compliments or endearments often fall into this category. (Plans for improving each of these skills will be presented later in this book.) However, when one partner responds with a willingness to please, the initial step has been taken. At this point, don't feel you need to agree on a plan that will teach the giving partner new skills required to satisfy. Both partners can simply appreciate the fact that an initial decision has been made to increase pleasant exchanges.

3. *Desires that you are able to address but do not want to.* Accept that your partner may not actually want to satisfy some of the things you ask, no matter how reasonable you may feel they are. Refusing to admit that one is reluctant to fulfill a partner's request may, in the long run, threaten the relationship, if it leads the giver to feel strong resentment, humiliation, anger or anxiety. Be very aware of the demands you are making of your partner and be sensitive to his/her hesitation.

4. *Desires that are unrealistic.* You may have expressed desires that could not be fulfilled even with co-operation of your partner. "Let's both quit our jobs and travel around the world." "Let's move to Hawaii." "I wish you would become a doctor." "I'd like to make love all day." "Ignore the children

and spend time only with me." These desires may simply be unrealistic for your particular situation.

Six: Decide who will attempt to satisfy first. Couples who are relatively satisfied will likely enjoy an exploration of new ways to fulfill each other's desires. Each is probably accustomed to deliberately attempting to make the other happy. Couples who are less satisfied will probably find this a more demanding exercise. These partners may think: "Why should I be loving when my partner has not been loving with me?" "Why should I put myself out? My partner hasn't made any effort." "I already feel that I give more." "I want my partner to demonstrate good faith by going first."

This game of "you go first" can result in a stalemate, unless both partners "go first." Each is then able to say "I will start to do the things that my partner has requested because I know that she/he will attempt to do the things I have requested." Self-disclosure and listening skills will make discussing planned changes and whether they are fair to each partner easier.

Seven: Be consistent and fair. You are almost ready to go into action. Remember that your objective is to be more loving and affectionate throughout your life together. Although you are more sensitive to your partner's desires, don't be tempted to go overboard trying to satisfy all of them right away. Overly generous givers can use up all their energy and enthusiasm in the first few weeks or months. Moreover, unless you are on a vacation when you begin your loving project, you will need to balance time with your partner with the other demands in your life. Finally, if one of you is overzealous, the other may find no room for the expression of affection.

Try to make roughly equal efforts to please each other. If you have requested breakfast in bed, it would be unwise for one partner to prepare the breakfast six days each week. If one partner has requested more time talking together, and the other more time doing a project together, a fifteen-hour project followed by an hour-long conversation might cause resentment. However, most happy partners find that for every affectionate gesture they offer they do not feel the need to receive a gesture of equal intensity immediately. Rather, happy couples enjoy an exchange of affection balanced over a period of time.

Eight: Learn to express love and affection verbally. Affectionate words, compliments, tokens of appreciation and sharing positive feelings can be rich and satisfying ways to exchange affection. However, we must learn to express our feelings verbally. If our parents were verbally affectionate, chances are that we will be, too. In many couples one partner is able to express verbal affection, while the other is not. However, if partners are willing to be flexible and patient, it is never too late to learn.

Roxanne, fifty-one, and Simon, fifty-three, decided to take a long, intense look at their love life when the last of their four children was soon to be off to college. Roxanne was feeling that their emotional exchanges of affection, which had generally centered on family activities, were becoming less frequent as their children grew older and more independent. She felt that Simon was becoming more committed to his successful business career and less available to her.

Roxanne strongly hoped that Simon could learn to be more demonstrative. She specifically requested that Simon attempt to show verbal appreciation through endearments and compliments. Roxanne's parents had been verbally affectionate with each other, but Simon had missed this type of exchange: his father died when he was five and his mother had never remarried. Although Simon strongly loved Roxanne, giving and receiving compliments made him very nervous. The private school he had attended reinforced the myth that any man who expressed affection was a sissy.

When Roxanne and Simon took a few moments to think of ways to express appreciation of each other, they had the following discussion.

ROXANNE: I'll go first.
SIMON: You had better. I'm not good at this.

ROXANNE: I like it when you cuddle me in the morning. I feel so close to you, and it's a great way to wake up!

SIMON: I'm surprised; I was afraid you didn't like our morning cuddles.

ROXANNE: Really?

SIMON: Because I thought that you thought I wanted to have sex, and I know you don't like to make love in the morning.

ROXANNE: Oh, no! It's just that I know there usually isn't time.

Roxanne and Simon had never talked about this habit; they were both pleasantly surprised. Such discovery of mutual pleasure can be one of the great advantages of partners expressing their appreciation of one another. Notice that applying listening skills made communication between Roxanne and Simon simple and direct.

The couple's next exchange struck a more sensitive note when Simon attempted to give a compliment.

SIMON: I like it when you wear a see-through negligée. It turns me on.

ROXANNE: I know you like see-through negligées, but that upsets me. I feel you like them, not me.

Roxanne had expressed the desire that Simon be more verbally appreciative. Simon was hesitant, but made an attempt because he wanted to please Roxanne. Instead of encouraging his offer of a compliment, Roxanne immediately responded to his self-disclosure with disapproval. If this exchange had occurred at home, Simon might have decided that "verbal-appreciation skills" were not worth the hassle, but in the course situation they could analyze their discussion.

Their objective had been to exchange positive impressions of each other's behavior. What might both of them have done to avoid the frustration? If Simon had said, "I like it when you wear a see-through negligée. You turn me on," he would likely have been successful in making Roxanne feel positive about herself and about him. As for Roxanne, it is her responsibility as receiver/listener to reflect on and appreciate the message.

80

Simon can help her by asking her how she feels about his compliment.

Simon and Roxanne returned to their discussion and conducted their exchange more easily the second time.

SIMON: So, how does my compliment make you feel?

ROXANNE: Well, I'm not sure. I guess I'm sort of glad that I still turn you on, and I would like to be more active in bed; but I know I would feel closer if we talked more.

SIMON: So, you like my compliment in part, and you figure we should talk more to have more fun in bed.

ROXANNE: Yes. Does it hurt you that I have mixed feelings about your compliment?

SIMON: No. I'm glad you told me, and I have a hunch that we're on the right track. I've already talked more about what I feel about sex than I have in years.

Other couples who resisted exchanging more verbal affection or appreciation expressed their objections as follows:

"Why should I give a compliment if I sense that my partner knows what I would say?" Never assume your partner knows what you are thinking or feeling unless you have told him/her. One of the major reasons for gradual reduction in couple satisfaction is that each partner takes the other for granted: "She always does the dishes." "He always gets up for the kids in the morning." "He always remembers to pay the insurance." Each of these actions makes the other partner's life easier, but need not continue only out of habit. Likely one partner will feel more positive about continuing a generous effort if she/he knows it pleases the other.

"If I make a conscious effort to give a compliment, it won't be a natural effort. My partner won't appreciate it because it won't have come from the heart." Make a positive statement about your partner's behavior or a characteristic only if it makes you feel good. Don't fake it! Spontaneity is a delicate thing, especially for couples who rarely verbalize their positive feelings toward each other: both giver and receiver can feel unnatural and awkward, as though they are programmed. However, it is

better for couples to feel strange for a short period while making conscious efforts to verbalize more of their positive feelings than to continue to feel estranged because they exchange few appreciative endearments. The initial awkwardness and stilted language usually disappear as each partner grows accustomed to giving and receiving compliments in words that come "naturally."

"I can't think of one positive thing to say about my partner, nor can I find a positive feeling to share. I'm really at a loss." Some people get so caught up in day-to-day life that they stop distinguishing pleasant events from mundane duties. Couples who face this problem might note the following list of verbal positives that other couples had exchanged during survival-strategy sessions. This list may help partners zero in on positive aspects of which they are unaware.

1. You make me feel sexy when you kiss me like that.
2. I like the way you put the kids to bed: you make them feel so protected and safe.
3. When you make supper, I feel you've gone out of your way to please me.
4. I am always impressed when I look at the paychecks we bring home. We've come a long way!
5. Your efforts to get into physical shape have really paid off. You look great!
6. I really appreciated how patient and caring you were during my illness. I felt looked after.
7. I'm glad you didn't blow up at me last night. Even though I made a fool of myself, you were very patient.
8. I appreciate you taking the kids on Saturday morning. It gives me a chance to get caught up on my reading.
9. I like it when you ask me questions about my work. I feel you're interested.
10. I felt great when you called me at work this morning, just to find out how I was doing.
11. I'm glad you decided to work with me on our communications skills. I feel loved when you invest in our partnership like that.

12. The sweater you knitted for me reminds me of the way I felt as a kid when Mum gave us all sweaters for Christmas.
13. Thanks for having the car checked. I was nervous with that shimmy and you know cars better than I do.
14. I really enjoy it when we get dressed up to go out for dinner. I feel we're not taking each other for granted.
15. I know you find going to my parents' place a hassle. I feel it's generous of you to come because they like you so much and I'm happy when we're all together.
16. Your taking that course was a great idea. You come home all enthused and we have great discussions together.
17. I really appreciate your sticking with your job. I know it's not easy. But your salary has made the difference between our living close to the line and being able to breathe a bit.
18. I love the way you listen to me even when I'm confused. I feel close to you and it helps me to make sense of the situation.

"It's not that I don't notice positive attributes – but I feel so angry at something my partner has done that I don't feel like saying anything about them." This stance is often taken by partners who are very frustrated with each other: "If my partner has done something that displeases me, I will refuse to mention something that pleases me." As we will discuss in Chapter Eight, expressing anger has an important place in intimate relationships. Some partners wait for their frustration to dissipate before they express affection or appreciation. They take the position that, "As long as I feel anger or disappointment, I cannot feel love." This is usually not true. Most of us can feel love and hate at the same moment. By expressing the anger only, we cheat our partner of reinforcement. Most couples can experience positive results if both partners make certain efforts. When one of you takes the position: "I will not say something positive until he/she changes to reduce my anger," the second partner is left without reassurance that the required effort is worthwhile.

Compliments or endearing words help a couple through the hard times. When both feel hurt after a fight and are wondering, "Is it worth it to be nice to someone who has made me angry?" the response should usually be yes.

If you make a plan to be more verbally affectionate, follow it through. Simon and Roxanne continued practising being verbally affectionate. Six months after they began, they summed up their progress as follows:

SIMON: Well, to be honest, I never thought I could be more affectionate. I figured at fifty-three, with my British background, it was too late to be the kind of affectionate husband Roxanne wanted. I felt Roxanne was only reasonable in hoping that I be more demonstrative, but I was afraid she had chosen the wrong guy. When told we could learn to be more affectionate I was still skeptical. When we started the exercises I figured we would fight because we would never be able to agree in a situation like this. And we did tangle a bit, but we sweated it out. I found pretty soon that we were having fun. One thing that really surprised me was that Roxanne was also a little shy at times. I even succeeded in making her blush with a few of my compliments.

ROXANNE: I knew he could learn if he put his mind to it. If you could know all the different problems Simon has faced in his life and how strong he is, you wouldn't be surprised at how well he tackled this challenge and how quickly he got over his shyness. Now he impresses me regularly.

But he wasn't the only one who had some learning to do. I realized that at times I had made it really hard for anyone to give me a compliment. I would laugh nervously or disagree. I never had trouble giving affection, but I realized that I was uneasy being on the receiving end.

I am much more satisfied with our relationship now. I no longer feel that Simon takes me for granted and I know just how much I mean to him.

Nine: Find new ways to express caring through actions.
Learning to share affection verbally can go a long way to make both partners feel more loved and appreciated; intimate partners have a whole range of loving alternatives available.

Couples who realize that their relationship has involved few nonverbal exchanges of affection sometimes have difficulty finding new modes of expression. Here is a sample of activities that couples use to bring them closer together. These range from simple evening activities to major projects and lifelong enterprises.

1. Give your partner a gift.
2. Participate in a sport together.
3. Go on a trip together – a simple two-hour excursion or a full-fledged vacation.
4. Enjoy a romantic dinner together.
5. Listen to music together.
6. Have a child together.
7. Redecorate a room; make plans for a new home.
8. Make love together.
9. Hug.
10. Garden together.
11. Share a joke.
12. Wear an article of clothing that makes you feel attractive and pleases your partner.
13. Take a course together.
14. Read a book or poem together.
15. Go to the cinema or the theater.
16. Spend time with interesting friends.
17. Introduce your partner to a new acquaintance of yours.
18. Share activities with your children.
19. Spoil your partner when she/he is feeling under the weather.
20. Give up a bad habit that irritates your partner – for example, rich food, cigarettes or alcohol.
21. Take walks together.
22. Play a game of cards.
23. Visit a museum or an art gallery.
24. Write a letter to a friend together.
25. Cook a meal together.
26. Look at photographs together.
27. Go to church or synagogue together.

28. Take a ride in the country together.
29. Meet for a drink or lunch as you would with an acquaintance.
30. Pretend you are courting again.
31. Designate one partner as the recipient of a special treatment for an hour, an evening or a day.
32. Make up after a fight.
33. Invite your partner's family to dinner.
34. Discuss a problem you are facing as parents and seek a solution together.
35. Support your partner during grief.
36. Tolerate a weakness that your partner cannot change.

Ten: Receive your partner's love and affection positively. As both partners attempt to be more affectionate and to fulfill requests, particular sensitivity is needed.

Listen to the discussion Rubin and Karen had the week after Rubin agreed to let Karen sleep in Saturday mornings; she, in turn, had agreed to be more available for listening to music and cuddling.

RUBIN: So, how was your Saturday morning?
KAREN: It was fine. I really needed the sleep. I wish we had made this agreement years ago.

Rubin did not reply, but was visibly offended. During the same week, after the couple had been listening to music for two hours and cuddling on the sofa, the following took place.

RUBIN: Shall we go and make love?
KAREN (*feeling hurt that Rubin had not noticed she had made the effort to please by listening to music with him*): I'm not in the mood tonight. I'm worried about my exam tomorrow.

Both spouses had made efforts to fulfill an expressed desire: Karen had listened to music with Rubin and he had kept their two children busy so Karen could sleep late on a Saturday. Yet each partner, as receiver of the caring behavior, missed an opportunity to show appreciation for the new efforts performed by the giver. Instead of saying thank you, they both demanded more: Karen by saying, "I wish it had happened sooner," and Rubin by requesting they make love. Each request – Karen's for sleep, Rubin's for more sex – was justifiable; however, bad timing destroyed any potential for positive results. If the couple failed to learn that each partner must offer immediate encouragement for new efforts, their progress would have come to a halt.

It is important that we show immediate appreciation for the efforts a partner makes to please us. This often requires a good deal of patience. Most of us can change our ways of relating to others, but only one step at a time. If we do not receive positive recognition for small achievements, change becomes difficult or sometimes impossible. Partners who exchange positive reinforcement infrequently will be particularly frustrated. They may say, "What my partner has just done for me is nothing compared to what I think I deserve," and come up with convincing arguments in support of this position.

However, if their desires are to be satisfied in the long run, partners must encourage all steps, however small, in the right direction. If the giver's efforts go unnoticed or are met with "It's about time," or "That's not enough," the giver can easily feel that it would be better to give nothing: "When I made my best offer I received criticism instead of appreciation."

Rubin and Karen could have expressed appreciation for what each had done instead of disappointment at what had not been done. When they went back over their conversation, they gave the needed positive reinforcement.

RUBIN: I'm really glad we found time to listen to music. It reminded me of what it was like when we first started going together. We used to just sit and listen for hours.

KAREN: It did me a lot of good, too. Just having time alone with you, taking it easy. And Saturday, I felt so much better after sleeping in. I really appreciate you taking the kids.

RUBIN: They wanted to wake you up, but once I got them moving we had a great time!

Eleven: Constantly vary loving exchanges. As we discussed in Chapter Two, one of the reasons couples become less satisfied with their marriage is "habituation." If an originally pleasing event is presented often enough it gradually loses its punch. Too much ice cream, too much sex or the same compliment too often decreases appreciation. This erosion of the power of pleasure is apparently not voluntary but is controlled by our physiological and neurological makeup. For an event to be effectively pleasurable, it must not occur too often, or else it must vary each time it occurs.

Unfortunately, many of us are not aware of this basic part of our nature. We expect the same lovemaking, compliments and tokens of affection to elicit the same response week in and week out. If couples had rated their overall satisfaction with their marriage annually, it would not be surprising to see ratings slowly drop year after year if steps were not taken to find new sources of pleasure. This slow erosion might go unnoticed until a comparison – either the early romantic phase of the relationship or the anticipated pleasure of a potential new partner – makes the dissatisfaction obvious.

There are several options available to partners at this point. The separation option, terminating a relationship that has "grown stale," is discussed in Chapter Twelve. Chapter Eleven explores open marriage: enlivening a relationship by expanding the sexual and emotional pleasure sources through other lovers. Partners need not resign themselves to thinking, "Life is supposed to be more boring as you grow older; intense pleasure is for the young."

Increasing the pleasure you share is possible: giving more verbal affection, improving your sensual expression together and increasing your shared positive activities all help. However, don't fall into the "same-old-thing" trap. Constant change is required to keep the "spice" in most intimate relationships. It is difficult to know when compliment, sexual pattern or shared activity has become routine. The best judge of the impact is the receiver.

You may say to yourself, "If my partner really loved me, she/he would notice that this compliment, this kind of kiss or this kind of gift no longer pleases me." Remember, your partner is not a mind reader. How can she/he gauge whether the gestures we intend to be caring have hit the mark? "If I say I'm bored, I will hurt my partner too much. Besides, I don't really know what would please me." It is during moments like this that it is worthwhile to repeat these twelve steps, updating your list, adding what would turn you on now.

You may feel that is too much work: an hour or two a month discussing new pleasures may seem long, especially if a couple is unused to having discussions of this sort. However, the time is a good investment without which pleasure drops and the pain, alienation and hostility increase. Besides, one or two hours per month – or even per week – is often considerably less than most couples spend watching television.

Twelve: Overcome attitudes that may block new efforts to exchange love. Two attitudes block some couples from putting their newly learned skills into practice:

1. *"Acting in a loving way will not make me feel more loving."* Couples who enjoy strong feelings of mutual love know that loving behavior and words engender loving feelings. Partners who are not satisfied with their relationship may think, "I don't feel very loving toward my partner now. I will wait until I feel more loving before I start acting or talking in a more loving way." In other words: "First change my feelings and then I will change my behavior."

Such couples will likely not be enthusiastic about the first eleven steps in this chapter; they believe the chapter started at the wrong place. However, "Change my feelings first then I will change my behavior" is part of the game of "You go first." It results in a stalemate and the relationship is the loser.

2. *"If we're in love now we'll be in love forever."* Couples who have been very satisfied and who experience frequent exchanges of love can become complacent about their love. They may believe that the love they receive and the love they feel represent something so strong that it will never change.

Partners who take their love for granted will not be attentive to subtle changes in their relationship. They may also be less tempted to follow the enhancement strategies I outlined because they feel they don't need to. But even very loving couples should be aware of subtle changes. Instead of taking your love for granted, some of the steps described above might strengthen that love.

In our culture we are accustomed to showing great perseverance, whether we are working hard, raising demanding children, studying to get ahead or exercising. We rate happiness in love as more important than health, career or even offspring; yet we are reluctant to accept that it takes thought, learning, perseverance, creativity and skill to maintain love between partners. Unless couples are willing to face the reality that a happy, healthy love is an achievement that demands effort and commitment, the present divorce rate is likely to continue its rapid rise.

5

Sexual Intimacy

Both Bob and Deborah are twenty-nine. He works as a bus
driver and she is a primary-school teacher. They had been
married five years and had a daughter of two and a son of
four. At home one Saturday night, when the children were
asleep, the following took place on the living-room sofa.

BOB *(placing his hand gently on her knee and looking her in the
  eye)*: Are you in the mood?

DEBBIE *(feeling suddenly tense)*: I'm not sure. I feel pretty tired.

BOB *(starting to worry that she will refuse)*: That's funny, I
  thought you slept well last night.

DEBBIE *(blushing)*: Well, I think I'd be too tired to get into it.

BOB: You're less and less interested these days. *(pause)* Is it
  because I lost my erection last time?

DEBBIE *(feeling guilty for not having accepted his invitation immediately)*: Why make a fuss about last time? I felt like
  sleeping anyway.

BOB *(feeling inadequate, unsure of his manhood and slightly
  angry that Debbie needed convincing)*: Well, I'm going to
  bed. See you later.

DEBBIE: *(Debbie followed him into the bedroom and took off her
  clothes.)* I'm willing to give it a try if you are.

Bob kissed her and pulled her to him. Debbie returned the kiss,
caressing his hair and face. Bob, feeling a firm erection,
moved above Debbie, who immediately stopped her caresses.
She tensed and lost her desire to make love and lay passively.
Bob attempted penetration but Debbie was not relaxed or
lubricated. Beginning to worry that he would lose his erection

if he didn't soon achieve penetration, he thrust harder. Debbie cried out softly with pain and closed her legs tightly.

BOB (*his erection considerably diminished*): Here we go again.
DEBBIE (*feeling no interest and some relief*): I'm sorry, dear, I guess I'm frigid.
BOB (*feeling out of control, unmanly, frustrated and angry*): Well, I'm obviously no magic lover, either, or you would be more excited and I wouldn't be impotent so often.

Bob and Debbie were referred by their general practitioner, whom Debbie had consulted for what she called "frigidity." Their sexual problems are very common, and both causes and treatment are known.

Common Sexual Problems

There are three common types of sexual problems encountered by women and three types frequently experienced by men.

Female Sexual Problems

Orgasmic difficulty: The woman does not experience orgasm during coitus with her partner. Many women are unnecessarily concerned about their inability to have an orgasm through intercourse alone. It is completely natural for some women to require manual stimulation of the clitoris before attaining orgasm.

A woman who has never experienced orgasm is said to have *primary orgasmic difficulty*. A woman who has been orgasmic but cannot experience orgasm at present is said to suffer *secondary orgasmic dysfunction*.

Dyspareunia: Pain may be experienced during penetration. The discomfort can occur at entry or when the penis penetrates more deeply.

Vaginismus: An involuntary contraction or spasm of the vaginal muscles due to extreme anxiety. This condition makes penetration impossible without severe damage to the vagina.

Male Sexual Problems

Erectile difficulty: Men may experience total or partial loss of erection prior to or during intercourse. Men who have never experienced intercourse, because they have erectile difficulty, are said to have *primary erectile difficulty*; those who have enjoyed normal coitus but now find it impossible on occasion are described as suffering *secondary erectile difficulty*.

Premature ejaculation: A man may be unable to delay his ejaculation until his partner is satisfied at least 50 per cent of the time.

Retarded ejaculation: A man may be able to penetrate but unable to ejaculate despite prolonged stimulation.

Frequency of Sexual Dysfunction

Until the 1960s sexual problems were regarded as medical illnesses and were thought to affect only a small portion of the population. However, research on normal and distressed sexual function[3] has demonstrated that sexual difficulties are very frequent indeed. It is estimated that more than 90 per cent of men experience erectile loss or premature ejaculation on occasion. Most women experience times when they are inorgasmic or experience painful coitus. While many people experience only passing frustration, various factors can cause a minor problem to take on greater proportions.

Causes of Human Sexual Problems

There are eleven factors frequently associated with the development of sexual difficulties. Each cause will be discussed separately, but most problems are triggered by a combination of factors.

Lack of Adequate Information about the Normal Human Sexual Response

Until recently, thanks in part to our Victorian predecessors, the public, professionals and scientists had little information, or worse, misinformation about human sexual response.[4] Without a fairly comprehensive knowledge of typical sexual response of men and women of different ages, couples may feel anxious about what is "normal" and may attempt ineffective sexual approaches. Frequently, misconceptions lead couples to frustrating and ineffective sexual behavior.

Male and female sexual responses are not identical. Problems arise when one partner mistakenly assumes that the other should respond as he/she does. The female excitation or arousal response usually takes longer than the male's; yet couples often rush sexual activity, particularly penetration, before the optimal moment for the woman.

Most men entering their first intimate relationship have already experienced orgasm through masturbation, and know what type of stimulation will lead them to orgasm. However, many women have not learned how to be orgasmic by the time of their first sexual relationship and begin only then to learn the types of sensual caress that lead them to orgasm.

Men generally experience orgasm during coitus; vaginal penetration provides the most intense stimulation. However, most women report that the most pleasurable sensations triggering orgasm come from direct caresses to the clitoris and surrounding regions.

Many couples do not realize that penetration and movement by the penis may not provoke intense pleasure to a woman's clitoral region. It depends on the anatomical makeup of the woman and how well the couple's bodies "match."

We cannot consciously control sexual arousal. Many people believe that their sexual response can be controlled at will. When, much to his embarrassment and his partner's displeasure, a man ejaculates a few seconds after penetration, both participants may wonder if he did it on purpose. When a woman fails to reach orgasm as soon as she would like or her partner loses his erection just before entry, either may think she/he is not trying hard enough. However, the human sexual response is not voluntary. We can decide when it is time to go to bed; but not when it is time to "get it up" or time to be aroused or time to come. In fact, one of the secrets to sexual pleasure is to relegate the mind to a very minor role.

Sex and aging. Many people assume that after a certain age we cease to desire sex and that the aged are incapable of regular sexual activity. In fact, couples can be active until their eighties and nineties if they are aware of how their sexual responses change with time. After menopause, women retain their capacity to lubricate and to achieve orgasm if they do not cease sexual activity. As men age, they do not lose their capacity to experience sexual pleasure, although direct intense stimulation of the penis is usually necessary for an older man to achieve a firm erection. A man may also find that he must wait longer between lovemaking sessions as he grows older.

Destructive Myths

There has been a good deal of misinformation about human sexual response transmitted in our culture, perpetuating erroneous beliefs and attitudes that can trigger or exacerbate sexual problems. Here are a few:

"We are born with an ability to have satisfactory sexual relations." In fact, we are born with the potential to experience certain sexual responses, but satisfying sexual activity requires partners who have gone through a variety of social and emotional learning experiences. An individual who has learned satisfying sexual behavior alone or with one partner will not automatically achieve satisfaction with a new partner. Couples must learn to have satisfying sexual relations together.

"A man who loses his erection is impotent and a woman who can't achieve orgasm is frigid. Both usually have physiological or deep psychological causes." Many individuals and, unfortunately, many physicians and other health professionals still call a man's difficulty to maintain an erection "impotence" and a woman's difficulties reaching orgasm "frigidity." These two terms should be scrapped: they are inaccurate and carry negative, unjustified connotations. In only a minority of cases will sexual difficulties be caused by physiological or deep psychological problems. Most of these problems are temporary, and stem from the way in which partners approach their relationship.

"If you love me, you'll know what I like." Many of us assume that our partner knows instinctively what pattern of sexual behavior will be pleasurable to us. However, most couples who consistently experience pleasure together constantly inform each other of their desires and responses. Mind reading works no better in bed than anywhere else.

"Mature women will experience vaginal orgasm." For centuries, it was assumed that the "natural" orgasm for a woman was achieved with penal thrusts into the vagina and that the "best" orgasm for a woman would occur in the vagina. Female orgasm does, in fact, occur in the vagina: the sensation of climax occurs when the muscles in the walls of the vagina contract rhythmically. However, few women will be brought to orgasm by a thrusting penis. Most women require direct or indirect stimulation of the clitoris to achieve orgasm.

"Masturbation is unnecessary, unhealthy, immoral and a sign of mental illness." Men and women who have not discovered their own sexual response through self-exploration often have great difficulty creating a rich sexual life with a partner, for masturbation is one of a variety of learning experiences through which full human response is developed.

A Spectator, Not a Participant

Both Bob and Debbie had fallen into a "spectator role," and were not sensitive to the pleasurable sensations derived from a romantic moment, a warm embrace, a caress. Bob and Debbie were attempting to give and receive sensual satisfaction; yet, because their efforts were unsynchronized, both were experiencing frustration. Debbie had a history of feeling tense about sexual relations. Only after at least half an hour of romantic caressing could she feel relaxed and aroused. She believed it neither normal nor fair to "take this much time," and she would rush herself, trying to keep up with Bob. Only on rare occasions was she lubricated before penetration. Instead of attempting to relax, she would mentally withdraw: "Oh, here I go again, I'm not ready, it's going to hurt."

After several sessions, Debbie learned to allow herself to become sufficiently aroused to approach orgasm but had not yet learned to let herself go. Instead of abandoning herself to the pleasure of the moment and asking Bob to continue his caressing, she would withdraw as before, observing her own response and expecting the worst – that she wouldn't come – or wishing she could have a vaginal orgasm.

Bob took on his "spectator role" just before penetration. Instead of being absorbed in giving Debbie pleasure, he became preoccupied with his own sexual response: "I wonder if my erection will be firm enough."

Anxiety Inhibits Sexual Response

Little boys regularly have erections in the first weeks of life, and little girls experience vaginal and clitoral swelling. Sexual arousal is natural, and a child will feel comfortable with it until a parent delivers a reprimand or a slap on the hand. When the child next moves to touch his/her genitals it may bring on an anxiety response: a quickening of the heart rate and tensing of the muscles. We are not born with anxieties; we learn them as we grow up, through interaction with others.

Bob was anxious that he was "not man enough to penetrate" or "not man enough to give Debbie an orgasm." He felt awkward touching Debbie's genitals with his hand and, especially, with his mouth. Debbie was almost always afraid that penetration would be painful. She was concerned that she could not give Bob enough pleasure. She felt that she should experience orgasm more often, but was shy to express her feelings about sex. Requesting a desired caress made her especially anxious.

We may be inhibited in intimate situations for any number of reasons. We may be self-conscious about our appearance, embarrassed to perform oral sex or other positions or awkward about making or refusing sexual invitations.

Guilt also Blocks Sexual Pleasure

Punishment of childhood curiosity about sex and of our early response to sexual impulses will teach us to be anxious in sensual situations. We may learn to feel very guilty about our sexual desires, and believe that our behavior is morally unacceptable. Many parents, clergy and teachers have preached that the main purpose of sex is reproduction, not enjoyment. This stops many of us from letting go with a partner: "I should not desire you," "I should not enjoy oral sex," "I should not masturbate," "I should not have fantasies about other partners," "I should not lose control," "I should not make too much noise," "I should not move too much."

Sexual Satisfaction and Open Communication Go Together

To consistently enjoy each other, partners need to develop a system of signals to communicate their preferences: how, when, how much, where. Not everyone will be aroused by the same stimuli; therefore, the art of achieving sexual satisfaction together is very much dependent on each partner signaling the other.

Bob and Debbie had not developed ways to communicate such information as when either was open to sensual contact; what types of precoital activities were desired or how long they might last; when Debbie was ready for intercourse; how Debbie could reduce the pressure on Bob and eliminate her own pain; or what types of caresses would heighten her chances of an orgasm.

Physical Illness and the Effects of Drugs

Certain sexual problems have been associated with physical disease and the use of drugs.[4] Reduction or loss of erection can be related to diabetes, circulatory difficulties or hormonal imbalance. Medication for hypertension and certain antidepressants can cause erectile difficulties. Usually, if a man has difficulty achieving a full erection before intercourse but not with caressing, while masturbating or upon waking in the morning, the cause is unlikely to be physiological. Rarely is premature ejaculation, the other most frequent male dysfunction, linked to physiological causes. Men concerned about this question should consult a qualified physician.

In women, the most frequent biological difficulty is *dyspareunia* (painful intercourse). Infections or, on rare occasions, physical anomalies can cause women to suffer irritation of the labia, which will make intercourse painful. Depending upon the angle of a woman's uterus and the size of her partner's penis, deep penetration can sometimes cause physical pain. Any illness affecting overall bodily health, certain drugs or any hormonal imbalance can affect a woman's responsiveness and limit her ability to lubricate and to experience orgasm. In general, vaginismus is rarely directly caused by a biological problem. Although vaginismus can be a rather frightening muscular spasm, it is usually caused by extreme fear of penetration. Women who experience painful intercourse or vaginismus would be well advised to consult their physicians.

Marital Discord

Obviously, satisfactory sex with someone with whom we are not feeling close or affectionate is difficult, if not impossible. Partners in conflict, however, are often surprised when their sexual appetite for each other drops radically. Many will find that when they feel hostile or distant, orgasms are difficult to achieve. Making love can be a good way to reduce hostility between partners, but not if ambivalent feelings are too strong. The delicate communication and co-operation that lovemaking requires are upset, if not destroyed, by anger and indifference. Sexual relations are vulnerable to sabotage by an angry or hurt partner: most of us know what sounds, movements or caresses might turn off our partner.

Lifestyle

Sex is a highly intricate form of play. Those who work around the clock can lose their ability to play. To make love comfortably, most couples need to be relaxed but not tired, free of time pressure and able to enjoy a rapport in a conducive atmosphere. Many couples develop sexual problems linked to an overly charged lifestyle: the demands of two careers, children, in-laws, sports and club activities, house repairs, financial problems, night courses, different work shifts and little time just to relax and talk.

Psychological Difficulties

To relax during sex with a partner, we need to feel secure, to share a certain trust. People who have experienced severe psychological trauma while growing up will have difficulty accepting themselves, let alone another person. General anxiety, extreme depression or thought disorder will interfere dramatically with the sexual response and make an intimate relationship with another person extremely difficult. A partner who suffers a severe psychological problem is best advised first to resolve the individual disorder before the couple attempts to improve their sexual functioning.

Change in Sexual Relations With Time

Most couples who have been together for a number of years find that their sexual relations are not as "wild" as during the initial stages of their relationship. This is natural and inevitable. Variation in types of sexual response and changes in intensity parallel the change in the love response described in Chapters Two and Four. A decline in the frequency and intensity of relations may cause alarm: are we no longer in love? One popular misconception claims that normal, happy couples make love an average of three times per week. In fact, the success of a relationship is not dependent upon how often a couple makes love. A couple who has intercourse six times a week will not necessarily be any happier than a couple who makes love once every two weeks.

Frequency of lovemaking depends enormously on other activities in the couple's life and what channels are open to sharing affection. Partners who share projects, laugh together, enjoy their children together, solve problems effectively and actively listen to each other have many styles of togetherness. To be fully understood, sexual relations must be viewed within the context of the whole relationship.

The Improvement of Sexual Relations

Thanks to pioneering discoveries made by Masters and Johnson,[4] sexual relationships are now improved through education. A couple can be helped to unlearn destructive anxiety and guilt responses and to learn more effective sexual behavior as they learn more about their sexual response, discard misconceptions and develop more realistic expectations of each other and of their relationship.

Even couples who have not encountered persistent sexual frustration might find that the procedures set out below improve their sexual relations, by offering ideas to experiment with in order to expand their repertoire of sexual relations.

Self-Exploration

To be able to enjoy a satisfying sexual relationship with a partner, we must feel comfortable with our own body, be free of tension and be unashamed of sensual pleasure. All sexual satisfaction is largely dependent on knowledge of our bodies. Women can learn more about their physical makeup through self-exploration, using the procedures listed below. To keep anxiety and guilt to a minimum, it is recommended that a woman try one or two new steps per session, for fear and guilt can be conquered only in small steps, not all at once.

Set aside thirty minutes to an hour, two or three times a week to follow the program. Be sure that you're alone and will not be disturbed.

1. Get fully undressed. Take a long, warm bath, washing yourself with your favorite soap and oils.

2. While you're in the bath, let your hand gently explore your whole body. Observe how your skin feels and notice which are your more sensitive regions – face, neck, ears, nipples and buttocks.

101

3. Wash and caress your genitals, exploring the various regions.

4. Get out of the bath. Dry yourself, again observing how the different regions of your body feel. Using a picture for reference, hold a mirror below your genitals and identify the different elements. Notice the outer lips of the vagina *(labia major)* and the inner lips (accessible by parting the outer lips). Notice the covering or "hood" of the clitoris just above the meeting of your inner lips. Gently pull back the hood to observe the clitoris.

5. Smooth powder or oil over your whole body. Then again concentrate on your genitals. Notice the differences in skin texture and how certain types of pressure and movements are more pleasurable than others.

6. Push your finger into the vagina, exploring gently while discovering what movements feel pleasurable. Withdraw your finger and notice the natural smell of the vagina.

7. Softly feel your breasts, buttocks, anal region, abdomen and genitals. Apply a lubricant or saliva to your clitorial region and vagina. With one hand, caress the genitals with movements. Repeat the most pleasurable movements in a rhythmic fashion, while using the other hand to caress other parts of your body. Do not attempt orgasm; just enjoy yourself.

8. Follow all of the above steps, rhythmically caressing your genitals, in particular the clitoral region, for as long as you find it pleasurable. As you become more excited your breathing will become heavy and you will likely feel your stomach, thigh and buttock muscles contracting. These are natural physical reactions to stimulation and will likely increase your pleasure and bring you closer to orgasm. As you become more excited, be aware that the movements you prefer around your clitoris change. Many women find that just before orgasm their clitoris is so sensitive they prefer to avoid direct stimulation, enjoying light and rhythmic caresses in the surrounding area. As you get near your climax, don't be surprised if you feel a loss of control or wish to cry out. Let yourself go. These experiences are natural and beautiful.

Exploration With Your Partner

Several interviews with Bob and Debbie revealed that neither knew what sexual stimulation Debbie found pleasurable, although both knew a lot about what Bob enjoyed. Debbie followed the steps summarized above and within three weeks found that she could regularly bring herself to orgasm.

The next step was to teach Bob what she had learned, through "sensate focus," a learning procedure developed by Masters and Johnson.[4]

Sensate Focus

Frustration in a couple's sexual relationship often stems from their becoming "too genital." The sweet words and caresses, seduction and teasing of courtship are often brushed aside when sex becomes a habit. The couple immediately "gets to the point" of intercourse and orgasm. However, the sexual pleasures of interaction can be blocked out by concentrating on the "end point," and gradually both partners can become less and less excited. Women particularly can suffer frustration with an overly genital approach to sexuality because they prefer slower and more total sexual experiences. As each partner becomes preoccupied exclusively with penetration and/or orgasm, he/she may become "spectators," as Bob and Debbie did.

"Sensate focus" is one way to break this pattern. The objectives of this exercise are to de-emphasize penetration and orgasm and refocus on sensation.

For a week or two, concentrate on tuning into what physical contact turns you on or off. Choose two or three moments in the week, preferably when you're fairly rested and relaxed but not tipsy. Slowly undress each other as you might have during your courtship. Try music and low lights.

One of you – the caresser – takes the role of the giver and the other takes the role of the receiver. The giver slowly explores thighs, calves, back, face, neck, buttocks and abdomen, while the receiver lies back and enjoys it. The receiver indicates verbally or nonverbally which caresses are pleasurable and suggests changes in pressure that would be more pleasant.

After ten or fifteen minutes, change roles. After you have both tried each role once, and before making love, talk about what you learned about each other's bodies.

Once you have learned about giving and receiving nongenital caresses, you can begin to teach each other about your genital pleasures. The man might prop his back up against the head-board with lots of pillows. The woman might then place her back on the man's stomach with her legs between his. The man can then fondle the woman's body slowly with her hand on top of his. When she feels ready, she will guide his hand down to her genitals and slowly show him the types of movements that she has discovered give her pleasure. Don't rush.

Remember, this exercise is not for bringing the woman to orgasm, but for her to teach the man the types of stimulation she enjoys. After she has had enough, the partners should change places.

Penetration and Erectile difficulties

Several weeks later, once you know more about your own bodies and how to communicate your pleasures, you can move on to intercourse. Remember that, ideally, your encounters will start with sensate focus. Don't begin actual intercourse too soon. The man might try lying on his back; the woman will then move above him with her legs apart so that she can lower her vagina onto his penis. One advantage of the female superior position is that once you are both feeling excited, the woman can control entry, slowly introducing the man's penis between her vaginal lips with one hand on his penis and the other on her vagina. This will allow the woman to control the speed, angle and depth of penetration, so she can avoid any premature or painful movements. The man, instead of having to ask himself, "Will I be able to penetrate?" or "Is she ready?" can relax and enjoy while the woman takes charge.

You may find it helpful – and fun – to use creams to reduce the friction of penetration.

Learn to Stop and Go

More than 50 per cent of North American men suffer from an inability to postpone their climax. You will recall Karen and Rubin, whom we met in Chapter Four. Karen had hoped that Rubin would become able to postpone his ejaculation. Rubin, much to his own dismay, usually ejaculated within a few seconds of penetration. After they had completed the sensate focus and genital focus, Karen and Rubin found the following technique helpful. Karen began caressing Rubin's penis manually. Rubin's responsibility was to monitor how excited he was becoming. Just before orgasm he noticed sensations that were very pleasurable, signaling that he was close to orgasm. As Karen's caresses brought him closer and closer to a climax, Rubin signaled her to stop just before he sensed that orgasm was inevitable. The two agreed on what the "stop" signal would be. Some couples use a word: "stop" or "wait"; others simply squeeze the lover's hand. While she waited for Rubin to cool down a bit, Karen caressed him gently but did not begin genital caresses until he felt he was no longer close to orgasm. Karen repeated this approach three or four times before allowing Rubin to reach orgasm.

After you have become comfortable with this procedure (probably after three or four sessions), try the same technique during intercourse. Adopt the coital position in which you both feel most able to stop movements that lead the man to ejaculate. Some couples prefer the female superior position; others are more comfortable with the man laterally across the woman. Most men find that the more relaxed they are, the longer they can postpone ejaculation.

If you choose a lateral position, the man should use a pillow to support his body so that he is free to concentrate on his sensation of inevitability. The woman might make genital movements to arouse, but he must tell her when to stop. Wait for his excitement to subside, then start the movements again. Allow him to approach orgasm three or four times, stopping early enough to prevent climax, before performing the final movements that trigger orgasm.

Female Orgasm

Many women find it difficult, if not impossible, to achieve orgasm through penal stimulation alone. It depends largely on the couple's physical makeup, and how their bodies interweave. I can suggest a few pleasurable ways to approach sensuality.

Any position from which the man can manually caress the woman's clitoris during intercourse is worth exploring. You might find that the female superior position will enable the woman to experiment with various movements while the man caresses her clitoral region. Some couples find other positions more suitable to freeing up the clitoral region for manual caresses. It may be more stimulating for the woman to control his finger or to use her own hand. If she doesn't come during intercourse, a couple should return to manual or oral caresses toward the end of the encounter.

Taking Turns

Sensuality is an exercise in giving and receiving. Some partners find it easier to give, others to receive. The exercises described in this chapter have been designed to help both partners become comfortable and effective in both roles. Temptation to end each encounter with intercourse must be resisted during the exercises. One partner must attempt to concentrate only on *giving* and while the other thinks only about *receiving*. The success of any plan to improve sexual relations requires a permanent, clean break with old patterns, or the old sources of trouble will reappear. Only with the total support and co-operation of both partners will the steps recommended for facilitating orgasm, erectile response or ejaculatory control work.

Reluctant Partners

One partner is often more motivated to improve sexual and sensual relations than the other. The keener partner may try a

106

variety of dangerous strategies to entice the reluctant mate into efforts to improve their sexual relationship: the "North-Pole treatment" (deny sex until the hesitant partner is ready to co-operate); the "teaser approach" (excite the partner but stop before satisfaction); dropping hints (" It could be better," "I've known better"); suggestive presents (a subscription to a favorite sensual review; a sexual-sensual improvement book, suggestive underwear); the "drive 'em crazy with jealousy" approach (well-timed flirtation to convince a reluctant partner to change his/her attitude); or withholding of essential resources (stop cooking meals or bringing home a paycheck), to name a few.

Although amusing on the surface, such behavior can be threatening to a partner and to a relationship. How to increase co-operation from a reluctant partner is relevant to all the survival strategies and is discussed in the last chapter.

Sex Therapy

The recommendations included in this chapter will help many couples improve their sexual relations. For certain problems, however, such as dyspareunia, vaginismus and persistent erectile difficulties, do not hesitate to consult a professional therapist to find the causes of the sexual frustration and the best solutions. Some of the approaches suggested here may be appropriate, but start with a professional diagnosis. Relationships are no longer doomed to infrequent, frustrating sexual relations and sex is a great way to share love.

6

Effective Problem-Solving

DAVE *(as he pays some outstanding bills)*: We're going to have to watch the budget, dear.

JEANNE: You don't think I already know? Every time I go shopping I skimp everywhere I can.

DAVE: Sure, and then you buy a twenty-five-dollar plant for your mother and a few toys that won't last the kids more than a week.

JEANNE: And just how much does your golf and curling cost us per week?

DAVE: They're tax deductible. Besides, you know the doctor told me to relax and to get more exercise.

JEANNE: But it needn't cost so much money, and he certainly didn't tell you to come home loaded from the club three nights out of four.

Sound familiar? This couple is grappling with problems all couples face: the family budget, leisure activities, gifts to family and loved ones and so on. As long as two people live together, they will have to make decisions and choices that affect both partners. Conflict is an inevitable part of intimacy. What distinguishes happy from distressed couples is not the number of problems they confront, but the style in which they solve their problems.

There are eight steps essential to effective problem-solving. Each step taken alone may seem easy; but you will likely find following all eight in sequence a little difficult at first, especially working as a couple. Remember, however, that most couples, even in a crisis, can learn to be more effective problem-solvers.

108

The Dangers of Ineffective Problem-Solving

Couples today have many more decisions to make than couples of previous generations: "Should she work?" "Should we have another child?" "Why aren't we making love more often?" "What contraceptive should we use?" "What will we do if we are both unemployed?" "Should we separate?" Our hectic lives can be very rich and satisfying if we decide wisely. Unfortunately, most of us have not acquired the basic skills of effective problem-solving before we enter a relationship. One partner might be a good problem-solver alone, but that is not enough. A couple, like a pair of skaters, is only as good as their combined skills. Because most couples haven't learned the basics of couple problem-solving, they tend to behave like Dave and Jeanne. Let us return briefly to their discussion and spot the mistakes that led to their ineffectiveness.

1. Poor timing: Dave was already hot under the collar about paying the bills.
2. Jeanne jumped in with, "I know already," instead of first agreeing with Dave that their finances were a problem.
3. Both Dave and Jeanne failed to acknowledge efforts that the other had already made to economize; instead, each one seized on expenses she/he resented.
4. Instead of trying to solve one problem at a time, they threw a number of issues in together once their argument had begun: their budget, Jeanne's buying a present for her mother and toys for the kids, the cost of golf and curling, Dave's health problem, his drinking.

The steps outlined in this chapter will help couples to spot these defects in their own problem-solving and to adopt more effective strategies.

Jeanne would be unhappy if Dave insisted she no longer give presents to her mother. Dave would be even less relaxed and more dissatisfied if Jeanne forced him to curtail his sports activities.

Ineffective problem-solving can be so frustrating that partners find themselves exchanging jibes or giving each other the silent treatment by the end of a discussion. Dave and Jeanne began their exchange with one central problem – mutual frustration over the budget – but within minutes they had touched off two new problems – Jeanne's resentment of Dave's lack of appreciation of her efforts to curb her spending, and Dave's awareness that Jeanne wanted him to give up his golf and curling although she was supportive of his looking after his health.

Before we outline the problem-solving strategies, bear in mind that, although they look complicated, most couples can learn them. A problem-solving "technique" may seem stilted and unnatural at first, but any feelings of awkwardness will disappear with a few weeks' practice. Most couples who seriously follow the eight exercise steps find that feeling unnatural temporarily is well worth it, if it ends the frustration associated with their old problem-solving.

Several hour-long sessions may be required to deal with the first problem tackled using this technique; but, with practice, couples can shorten the sessions considerably. As well, once problem solving has begun, benefits are reaped immediately, while the consequences of inadequate solutions will be felt for hours, days and sometimes years.

How to Solve Problems Effectively

1. Play on the same team.
2. Choose the right moment.
3. Pick a problem.
4. Define the problem clearly.
5. Have a brainstorming session.
6. Evaluate your proposed solutions.
7. Make a decision.
8. Put your solution(s) into action and test its (their) effectiveness.

1. Play on the same team. Most couples, like Dave and Jeanne, sincerely love each other and want to make a success of their relationship. But when they approach their problems, they become adversaries. Even happily married couples tend to be more critical of and difficult with their own partners than they are with strangers. Remember that you are both on the same team. If what you do hurts one partner, you both lose. The trick is to find a way to grapple with the problem that will allow you both to come out on top.

"Problem-solving" and "fighting" are not the same thing. Fighting, where certain simple rules of fairness are respected (see Chapters Eight and Nine), can be very healthy for a relationship. However, couples in successful relationships have learned to separate their fighting from their problem-solving.

In Chapter Eight we will discuss couples who fight too much ("hawks") and couples who do not fight enough ("doves"). Hawks often bicker over their differences day in and day out; doves deny that problems exist. They tend to respond to conflict with avoidance ("Oh, you know best dear," or "I'm sure it won't happen again"), denial ("Oh, it's really not that important"), fatalism ("That's life") or taking too much responsibility ("It's my fault"). Often doves need to be made aware of their differences before they can begin to discuss them.

Doves usually believe three myths about problems between partners: "Problems only arise in couples who are in severe trouble." "We never disagree on small points, but if we ever face a real problem, we'll know how to solve it." "Problems are best ignored." Each of these myths can lead the dove couple from "total bliss" to intense conflict in a surprisingly short time.

2. Choose the right moment. Hawks, such as Dave and Jeanne, need to work on their timing. This demands a certain self-awareness from both partners. Choose a time for problem-solving when both partners feel least aggressive, when you will be able to approach your problem calmly and clear-headedly.

Dave discovered that he should not attempt problem-solving with Jeanne immediately after paying bills, coming home from work or having a few drinks. Jeanne found that her hardest times were when she was feeling low and after a rough day at university.

Avoid distractions such as television, visitors, children, in-laws and friends. Don't attempt problem-solving before or while sharing a meal. Take enough time that you won't feel rushed, so that both partners have equal opportunity to express fully their feelings about the problem at hand. To be effective problem-solvers, most couples need at least one hour of uninterrupted time, especially when they are first learning the skills. Recording your problem-solving sessions in a notebook is usually a good idea.

3. Pick a problem. You're ready to go. Unless you've both been living in a vacuum for the last few years, you shouldn't have any trouble finding a problem to begin practising on. But be careful how you define your problem. Make sure you don't take on an issue that is too painful for either of you.

Each of you divide a sheet of paper vertically in three sections. List the problems you would like to discuss with your partner on the left-hand side of the page. Assess how difficult it would be for you to discuss the problem on a scale of one to ten (one being "easy" and ten being "impossible"). Your partner will fill in the right-hand column later.

Here is the problem list Dave compiled:

List of problems

Problem	Difficulty for me	Difficulty for my partner
Budget	8	
Giving gifts to mother-in-law	6	
My drinking	7	
Losing my job	6	

Exchange lists and assess the difficulty of dealing with the problems listed by your partner.

Why go through all this? Why not just agree on a problem and avoid wasting so much time? Couples who don't take the time to understand their problem before discussing it risk reducing their problem-solving session to a fight session. If you begin with a difficult or moderately difficult problem (a score from six to ten), you are trying to run before you have learned to walk.

Remember that your objective is to learn how to function as an effective team. Don't worry that you may be able to do these "exercises" but not be able to solve real problems. These skills can be applied to matters of crucial importance: Is an open marriage a viable alternative? Should we both keep working? Is separation the best solution? The more difficult the problem, the more you will need effective problem-solving techniques.

As you learn these new skills, you will want to apply them to your more difficult problems. And remember, almost all couples, whether happy or distressed, lack and must learn effective problem-solving skills.

4. Define the problem clearly. It may seem surprising that two people who have lived together for months, years or even decades often think they're discussing the same thing while talking at cross-purposes. When Dave began the discussion quoted above with, "We're going to have to watch the budget," Jeanne seized on the topic, thinking she knew exactly what he was talking about. Some of the confusion and frustration that ensued could have been avoided if they had taken the time to define the problem before voicing their feelings.

Answering these questions can help you to define a problem well:

What is the problem? Dave and Jeanne need to establish just what it is they are talking about. What is their budget? How much money comes in? How much goes out? How much is spent where?

When does the problem occur? Is David worried about money every day? Or is he only concerned when bills are due? Is he worried about their present financial situation or about the future? ("Things aren't going too well at work. What will we do if I lose my job?" or "Jeanne wants to keep studying. I don't know that we can afford it," or "Christmas is coming and we always spend a fortune on presents.") Is Jeanne worried about their monthly budget, the fact that Dave's paycheck

113

doesn't seem to stretch far enough or merely about the cost of his golf-club membership?

Whom does the problem involve? One partner, the other, both, a third party? Rarely is a problem or solution confined to one partner. For example, if your partner smokes and wants to quit, define the situation, from your point of view, in these terms: "How can I help my partner stop smoking?"

How does each partner feel about the situation? Angry, frustrated, depressed, anxious? Describe your feelings honestly and clearly but briefly, especially if you are a hawk couple. This question is not intended to precipitate a fight; it is an opportunity for each partner to indicate how important the problem is to her/him.

Be diplomatic in defining the problem. It is crucial that each of you feels you have had the chance to answer these four questions and that your partner has understood your answers. The following list of things to do and to avoid will prove helpful at this stage of the problem-solving exercise:

Do	*Don't*
Listen carefully to your partner.	Don't interrupt your partner.
When your partner has presented a point, summarize what was said and have your partner verify your summary.	Don't assume you have understood her/his point if you haven't summarized and verified.
Stick to one problem at a time. Should you find that your initial choice is, in fact, several problems, name the secondary problems and decide on one as the topic for the session.	Don't try to solve more than one problem at a time.
Stay in the present. Talk about what you can change today and tomorrow, not what you could have done yesterday.	Don't dredge up past issues or disagreements.

(continued on next page)

(continued)

Remember to *understand* does not mean to *agree*. Although you might not agree with your partner on answers to the four questions, you can show respect by listening and trying to understand.	Don't disagree outright with your partner's definition of the problem.
Keep your answers short.	Don't dwell too long on your own answers to the questions; don't hog the floor.

Be sure your final definition is specific. Check it by asking the questions above. Here are a few examples of problems and the specific definitions couples formulated by answering the four questions.

Initial problem	Final definition
We need to tighten our budget.	I think you spend too much money on gifts for the family, and I think I'm going to lose my job. What can we do?
Your golf and curling cost a fortune and you come home drunk.	I think you drink too much. What can we do together to solve this problem?
I feel hemmed in.	I want an open marriage and you don't. What can we do?
You're a lousy father.	I feel you could discipline the children more. What should we do?
You never cook me dinner anymore.	I wish you would cook dinner more often – you used to. What can we do?
You take my working for granted.	I feel you expect too much from me at home while I am working full-time. What can we do?

5. Have a brainstorming session. Once you have specified your problem, write your definition at the top of a blank page in your notebook. Ask yourselves, what are some possible solutions? Follow these guidelines while you are answering this question.

Let your mind go. Present any solution you think of, even if it seems ridiculous. The more inventive you are the better are your chances of finding a viable solution.

Don't criticize any solutions proposed at this stage. Avoid saying: "That will never work." "We've tried that before." "Aren't you forgetting something?" "That's not realistic." Later, both of you will have plenty of time to evaluate the pros and cons of any solution you decide is worth discussing.

Be positive. For example, instead of proposing that your partner be "less cold and distant," ask her/him to be more affectionate. If you want your partner to take a greater part in managing the finances, try saying "You could do the books with me" instead of "You could stop leaving the budget to me alone." It is always easier for an individual to change her/his behavior in a new and positive way than to concentrate on eliminating an annoying habit.

Clarify proposed solutions. If you're not sure what your partner means, help him/her to spell out the proposed solution by asking questions, summarizing and verifying.

Dave and Jeanne came up with the following problem definition and this list of potential solutions in their brainstorming session:

Problem Definition	Possible Solutions
At the end of the month we invariably have less money than we need to pay our bills. We don't want to take out yet another loan. What can we do?	Dave quits the golf club. Jeanne cuts her spending on gifts by half. We prepare the monthly budget together. Dave applies for a promotion. Dave takes a full-time job, which could include nights and some weekends.

(continued on next page)

(continued)

	We spend our vacation at home instead of taking a long, potentially expensive trip.
	Dave cuts down his drinking at the golf-club bar.

6. Evaluate your proposed solutions. Now look at the pros and cons of each alternative that seems worthwhile.

Review your list and cross off any alternatives that you both agree are completely unrealistic. In some cases one of you will think a proposition is worth considering, while the other would prefer to eliminate the solution without discussion. In the spirit of good faith, spend some time evaluating this type of alternative. Otherwise the partner whose opinion has been overruled may hold a grudge throughout the entire session. Remember that discussing an alternative does not mean that it will be the solution you select at the end of your problem-solving session.

Discuss the remaining alternatives on the list one at a time. What are:

the advantages from your partner's perspective?
the advantages from your perspective?
the disadvantages from your partner's perspective?
the disadvantages from your perspective?

Take turns being speaker and listener. For example, while Dave enumerates the disadvantages of quitting golf, it is Jeanne's responsibility to listen carefully. She can then summarize her reading of Dave's argument and ask him to clarify any aspect she finds unclear. Dave won't try to convince Jeanne that he is right in seeing certain disadvantages to the solution and that she is wrong not to see the situation as he does. Similarly, Jeanne will suppress any immediate urge to change Dave's mind about the golf club.

Remember, a couple is made up of two separate people who are very different in certain ways. It's only natural that each partner will have different preferences for different reasons. List in your notebook the advantages and disadvantages each of you see in your selected proposals.

Dave and Jeanne prepared this chart for their suggestion, "We prepare the monthly budget together."

Possible Solution: We prepare a budget together once a month.			
DAVE		JEANNE	
Advantages	*Disadvantages*	*Advantages*	*Disadvantages*
We would both know exactly where we stand each month.	Time wasted – it takes only one person to do the books.	We would both have the same information to go on.	We may fight while preparing a budget together.
I would feel that Jeanne is behind me.	I wouldn't be able to fool myself about money I'd like to spend on luxuries such as drinking at the bar.	We wouldn't fight every month when the bills get paid because we'd both know where we stand.	We would have to admit that we must cut back on luxuries like extravagant gifts and booze.
I would be forced to acknowledge that I don't have the money for luxuries.	It will take Jeanne a while to learn the bookkeeping system.	I would feel that Dave trusted me with our finances.	I am not very good at bookkeeping. Who would keep the kids out of the way?

Once you have listed the pros and cons of each alternative, turn back to your list of possible solutions. Rate the desirability of your alternatives, each partner assigning a number from one (undesirable) to ten (highly desirable) to each proposal. Here are Jeanne's and Dave's ratings of their solutions.

Possible solutions	Desirability	
	DAVE	JEANNE
Dave quits the golf club	3	6
Jeanne cuts her spending on gifts by half	6	3
We prepare the monthly budget together	7	7
Dave applies for a promotion	6	7
Dave takes a full-time job, which could include nights and some weekends	9	1
We spend our vacation at home instead of taking a long, potentially expensive trip	8	7
Dave cuts down his drinking at the golf-club bar	10	10

7. Make a decision. Ask yourselves, "Can we decide on the best solution to this problem today?" Each of you should answer this question. Verify your understanding of each other's answer and clarify any confusion.

Don't expect all of your solutions to be workable. After following steps one through seven, you may generate a solution that both find highly desirable. However, it is more likely that no single solution thrills you both but a few satisfactory solutions don't seem too objectionable to either of you.

Find a solution that lets you both "win." The art of choosing a successful solution is finding one that is satisfactory to both of you. If you give a solution a desirability score of eight, nine or ten while your partner rates the same possibility as a one, two or three, this solution is not the ideal choice. Such a lopsided option would increase one partner's happiness while diminishing the other's. In a relationship, if one loses and the other wins, you'll both be losers before long.

Dave's brother had suggested that Dave manage the family shoe store. This would have increased Dave's revenue significantly but he would have to work days, evenings and weekends. Dave liked this alternative very much, but Jeanne was strongly against the long hours. Dave agreed to drop the option.

You may find that several options together provide the best solution. Dave and Jeanne opted for several choices on their list. Both agreed to exercise a degree of self-control. Dave didn't want to give up his evenings at the golf-club bar but offered to give up drinking, which satisfied Jeanne. Jeanne offered to do her part by halving the cost of her presents to her mother and the kids. They agreed to give joint budget sessions a try

You may come up with a new alternative while talking about your original selection. While Jeanne and Dave were discussing the possibility of Dave working in the family store, Jeanne suggested she work three days a week. She had been toying with the idea of taking part-time work for a while and added this alternative to the list. Dave was delighted.

You may not succeed in finding an alternative that satisfies both of you. A stalemate will result when a couple has an accumulation of unsettled problems. Frustration is understandable; but, instead of giving up or allowing your problem-solving session to degenerate into an altercation, look for a compromise. A successful relationship is built on compromise brought about by effective negotiation. Unfortunately, many of us have not yet learned to give and take. (In the next chapter we will discuss negotiation tactics that foster effective compromise, and those tactics to avoid at all costs.)

8. Put your solution(s) into action and test its (their) effectiveness. Pinpoint your best chances of success. (You may need the negotiation skills described in Chapter Seven if you are resolving a stalemate.) Then formulate a plan of action.

1. Write the solution you have agreed upon in your notebook.
2. Ask yourselves: what is to be done? by whom? where?

when? These questions will reveal any significant details you have omitted while solving the problem.

3. Don't be hard on yourselves: you cannot foresee all the details, all the time. As you get closer to putting a solution into effect, unanticipated minor or even major problems may arise.

As they recorded their solutions, Dave and Jeanne found they had missed several points. Who would collect the bills? Who would list future expenses? Who would keep the records? When would they have an interference-free hour or two to spend on the budget? Once raised, each of these questions could be answered quite easily.

Evaluate the effectiveness of your solution. Try your new solution for a set time – a few days, a week or a month. At the end of your trial period ask yourselves, "What are the strengths and weaknesses of our solution as it stands now?" Don't be surprised if all does not go according to plan, especially if problem solving is new to you. Using your listening skills, discuss the results of your efforts and decide whether you should attempt the same solution again. If so, with what, if any, modification? If not, should you conduct a fresh problem-solving session?

Dave and Jeanne put into effect their decision to plan a budget together. Their first, hour-long meeting ended in frustration: few figures were down on paper and Jeanne had several "upsetting surprises." They had more debts than she had suspected, and their monthly expenses exceeded their income. A second hour of discussion would have been ideal, but they were interrupted by unexpected visitors. The following week they picked up where they had left off and realized that the exercise was "not so bad once all the problems they faced were out in the open." Both welcomed the prospect of Jeanne's part-time work bringing in additional revenue.

Their golf-club-bar-bill solution was more difficult to implement than either had expected. After several attempts to leave the club immediately after his golf game, Dave realized he found it difficult to resist temptation. His golfing partners almost invariably insisted that he not be a "party pooper"; a few post-game drinks relaxed him and he enjoyed the clubhouse banter.

Dave and Jeanne tackled the question, "How can Dave resist the pressure to have a drink at the golf club?" They finally decided that Dave would stay for a drink at the club at most one day out of two. The days he left immediately after his game he would explain that he had made plans to be with his family. The days he stayed he would stick to orange juice or a single beer. This strategy worked according to plan.

Their plan to cut Jeanne's spending on gifts also required some adjustment. She had made promises to both her mother and the children. "How can I tell Mom and the kids that the expected gifts won't arrive?" Jeanne and Dave opted for honesty as the best policy and Jeanne met with less resistance than expected when she put this solution into effect.

Many couples expect, unrealistically, that one problem-solving session should eliminate the need for all future discussions; yet couples rarely solve their problems on the first attempt. Gradual improvement through "successive approximations" is more likely. If the steps outlined above are followed, modification of solutions rather than returning to square one usually does the trick. Day-to-day adjustments can be arranged through brief discussions.

Dave and Jeanne were delighted with their new skills. They found problem-solving procedures effective in dealing with economic problems, as well as problems and clashes related to Dave's job, their vacation and the children's education. They discussed Jeanne's part-time work according to the same rules.

Jeanne put it this way: "Before we developed our problem-solving techniques I would dread discussions about our problems. We would invariably end up either fighting or avoiding each other completely for hours afterward. Now we can settle most issues without argument. I wouldn't say we've solved all our problems, but now, when we don't agree, we know why, and we don't waste a lot of time trying to talk about ten problems at the same time."

Dave added, "I had never thought we could be so level-headed. We used to just let things build up until they blew up. Using the problem-solving techniques, we usually find a workable solution to a problem or, at least, a temporary one that prevents too much damage."

When to Tackle the Big Problems

Begin with only mildly difficult problems to familiarize yourselves with this new procedure. After the eight steps have been mastered on simple problems, more difficult issues could be tackled. Couples invariably find that, as the subject material "heats up," following the rules becomes increasingly difficult. Restrained discussion can give way to courtroom-style debate. However, the eight rules become increasingly valuable with the difficulty: abandoning them means returning to inefficient and painful tactics.

Can All Problems Be Solved
Through Problem-Solving?

Definitely not. The success of problem-solving depends on the personalities of the partners involved, how they interact, what problems they face and what solutions, if any, they can select to help them to be happier together.

If one partner is feeling lost or confused, a session of active listening, not problem-solving, is required. In other instances, problems can be assuaged with a loving gesture or shared sexual intimacy. Solutions to some problems can only be found through negotiation and compromise.

Sometimes it is better to fight than to solve problems. (See Chapters Eight and Nine.) Later, we will discuss applying problem-solving procedures to issues modern couples frequently find extremely difficult to handle: how to divide work within and outside the home so neither partner feels cheated, and how to solve issues related to extramarital relationships and separation. Most couples who have practised the eight problem-solving steps outlined in this chapter on their simpler problems find that they are much better prepared for the more challenging ones.

7

The Art of Negotiating Effective Compromises

It takes two to make a couple, two separate individuals. Although they might share certain ambitions and tasks, some of their preferences and their expectations of their relationship are bound to differ. She prefers city life; he loves the idea of living in the country. He would enjoy an evening at the baseball game; she would prefer to go to the ballet. She adores the beaches of Florida; he prefers a European vacation. He wants the children educated in France; she wants them to go to an English school. She thinks marriage should involve plenty of "dialogue"; he prefers "actions." He enjoys active sex; she prefers slow caresses. She wants a monogamous marriage; he prefers an open one. He feels he should be the dominant partner; she prefers an egalitarian relationship.

These examples do not, of course, belong to one relationship, but in all cases, the partners succeeded in resolving their conflicting interests to their mutual satisfaction.

Before you read any further, write down ten things about which you and your partner see eye to eye and ten issues about which you differ.

Couples deal with their differences in one of three ways.

"We have no differences." Some couples deny they have ever clashed over any significant issue. Such claims are generally untrue: even highly compatible couples have some important differences. Both partners of a dove couple carefully navigate around their differences for fear that any admission of conflict would be saying "I don't love you." Those who take this head-in-the-sand approach run a terrible risk. One or both partners may eventually surface to find that once-small problems have become monumental and, perhaps, insoluble.

"We should be the same." Other couples fight constantly over their differences. Neither partner can accept that the other is not made in his/her image; each punishes the other for being different. This "hawk" couple is described in more detail in Chapter Eight.

"How can we resolve our differences?" A third type of couple admits that their preferences and expectations are not the same. Instead of burying their heads in the sand or declaring war, they attempt to resolve conflicts in a mutually acceptable fashion. The techniques of negotiation and compromise that have been effective in helping partners come to terms with their differences are set out below.

Negotiation: When two partners have admitted that their differences are causing conflict, they may choose to evaluate the situation together and examine potential solutions, with the object of resolving their conflict in a way that is acceptable to both. Usually, not always, the best solution is a negotiated compromise.

Compromise: The couple may, during their negotiation, come up with several possible solutions. When they choose a solution by which the gains and losses of both partners are equal, they have compromised. Not all compromises work. A satisfactory compromise will improve the relationship by allowing both partners to gain more than they lose. A compromise will be ineffective if one or both partners lose too much; in the long run, it will reduce the quality of the relationship.

Why Many Couples Avoid Negotiation and Compromise
Many people resist negotiation or compromise for any of a number of reasons. One of the following excuses is typically put forward by partners to justify their reluctance.

"We don't need to negotiate; we always agree." Ostriches and highly compatible partners take this stance. The ostriches avoid confrontation even though they have critical differences. Unfortunately, ignored problems grow and often eventually explode.

Highly compatible partners are lucky in many ways. They share many opinions and preferences. These partners don't need to negotiate as often as partners who are less alike, as they rarely experience conflicts over important issues. However, compatible partners who never learn to negotiate may be ill-prepared when they do find themselves differing.

Many of life's expected and unexpected events and crises can generate conflict: aging, sudden illness, unemployment, a new job, a child leaving home, one partner making a new friend the other does not like, even a new hobby. Suddenly "the perfect couple" who appeared to be "so happy together" have separated. They were happy, until they had to face a problem that demanded negotiation skills they had never developed: their first "important" difference turned out to be irreconcilable.

"Negotiation is fine in a business situation but it would depersonalize our intimate relationship." The word "negotiation" scares off many couples. Some assume that negotiation between partners is like bargaining between management and unions or employer and employee. Experts in both areas operate on principles that could profit the others; but many labor-management negotiation tactics should be employed only by couples planning to separate.

Negotiation between partners does share three basic characteristics with management-employee negotiations. Bargaining is necessary, because the parties concerned have strong differences of opinion on important issues. Conflict must be resolved through a solution acceptable to both sides. If a suitable compromise is not reached, one or both parties will suffer.

Negotiation between partners need not be dehumanizing. In fact, it can be an amusing, even exciting exercise that helps partners share warmth and understanding. The success of negotiation between partners depends on how the couple approaches the resolution of their differences.

"Negotiation would take the magic out of our relationship." Some couples avoid negotiation and problem-solving because they are afraid that confrontation and haggling over a problem would destroy romance. However, few couples perpetuate the absorbing passion of "falling in love" unless they see each other but once a month. In most cases, if partners do not learn negotiation skills, not only will the "magic" disappear, but they may wake up to find that they can no longer tolerate each other.

Negotiation, when carried out sensitively, can increase the "magic" of your relationship. Problems that distract from the romantic aspects of your life together get solved. New compromises may actually make you and your partner happier; you may feel closer to each other when your differences are admitted and resolved.

Timing is crucial for effective negotiation; sessions should be restricted to certain times and specific locales. Do not attempt to discuss a problem during sexual play, a romantic dinner, an outing with the children or a relaxing vacation. Schedule your negotiation sessions so they do not infringe on those precious "magical moments."

"Why negotiate? I've got things the way I want them." If one partner is deriving most from an arrangement, she/he may believe that nothing can be gained from negotiation: the husband who does not want his wife to work or to share in the formulation of a budget; the wife who refuses to discuss a sexual problem or to allow her husband to develop closer ties to their children. Not all stalemates of this type can be resolved through negotiation, but it's usually worth a try.

"I'm too angry to discuss our differences." Negotiation requires that both partners keep a lid on their anger. A negotiation session is not a fight. If one or both partners' feelings of anger are so strong that they cannot respect the rules of fair

negotiation, a good, fair fight may be more productive. Once the pressure has eased a bit, they can resume negotiations.

Some partners express their anger by griping and criticizing. A negotiation session can begin quite successfully with a gripe or a request for change; but criticism must then give way to negotiation strategies such as brainstorming, listening or suggesting compromises. Negotiating when angry or discouraged takes practice. A person who is exceptionally frustrated or quick to attack or criticize may find it difficult to exercise the self-control required for successful negotiation. Such a person might honestly believe that her/his partner has hurt her/him so often and so much that it is up to the partner to change or to offer to compromise before he/she does. Both spouses saying "You go first" is not conducive to negotiation. The "I'll not give you what you want because you won't give me what I want" stance has the same effect. Partners in a stalemate are not likely to enjoy a satisfying relationship.

Negotiation in Good Faith

Good-faith negotiation requires that both partners work hard to find a solution to their difference that will satisfy both partners. It is important for partners to acknowledge that it is rarely in the best interest of the relationship to adopt a solution that satisfies one partner and causes the other to lose: it may be necessary for one partner to accept a solution that is not his/her first choice but is acceptable to the other.

"But," says the person who is used to defending her/his own interests, "why should I be the one to suffer? My partner rarely makes a sacrifice on my behalf." Reciprocity, the final element in good couple-negotiation techniques, answers this objection: "I know that if I work hard to make you happy – by abandoning my preferred solution and accepting a compromise solution that you can accept comfortably – and you work by the same principle to make me happy, we will both be happier in the long run." This attitude breaks the who-goes-first stalemate because the partners say, "We'll both go first."

How to Negotiate Fairly

One: Start easy. If you want to learn how to work as a couple and you have little experience, it is best to practise on a relatively easy problem, an issue that does not cause too much tension. Otherwise you may find that your session degenerates into a less than fair fight or silent anger.

Two: Brainstorm to come up with possible compromises. Negotiation starts where problem-solving leaves off. You and your partner may have followed the problem-solving steps outlined in Chapter Six. You successfully came up with positive solutions to a problem only to find that you cannot agree on a solution acceptable to you both. This is the time to look for compromise solutions.

The experiences of Allan and Marcia illustrate these steps well.

Allan's negotiation session.
Marcia feels that Allan spends too much time (seven to ten hours per week) jogging with his friends. Allan would like Marcia to get into shape. She has no exercise program.

After brainstorming during a problem-solving session, the couple came up with the following list of potential solutions.

Potential solutions	Level of desirability	
	MARCIA	ALLAN
Marcia joins the jogging club five nights a week	1	10
Allan gives up jogging three nights a week	10	1
We play tennis together three times a week	5	4
We take aerobic dancing together	10	3

None of the solutions generated was initially mutually acceptable, yet Allan and Marcia learned several principles of negotiation and compromise that helped to break the impasse.

It may be possible to combine two solutions or to modify one solution so that it becomes acceptable to both partners. For example, after some discussion, Allan decided that he would be willing to play tennis twice a week if he could still jog at least four times a week. If Allan kept on jogging after work at his club, this alternative would still have put a big strain on Marcia. So Allan offered to jog before breakfast or at lunch, so he would be free to play tennis with Marcia two evenings a week and to spend more time with his family during dinner hours. This combination and modification of proposed solutions satisfied both partners.

Sometimes, discussion about the advantages and disadvantages of proposed solutions reveals the need for an entirely new solution. For example, Marcia was more active walking and bicycling in the summer, but she confessed that she needed a "bit of a kick in the pants to stay active during the colder months." Allan hated to jog in the winter but loved to jog during the summer. Because their preferences differed so drastically, they had to come up with an entirely new solution to effect a compromise. They decided that, during winter weeks, Allan would jog twice, they would play tennis together once, they would take aerobic dancing together once and Marcia would do aerobic dancing alone once. In the summer, they would drop the dancing and Marcia would bicycle beside Allan on his long runs twice a week.

In some circumstances, the most successful compromise allows one partner her/his preferred solution to one part of the problem and the other partner his/her preferred solution to another aspect. What counted most for Marcia was that Allan's jogging not take him away from the family. Allan offered to stop jogging after work and instead run at noon so he would be available at supper times to help with the cooking and be with the family. In exchange, Marcia agreed that Allan would have one long run with his old club on Saturday afternoon while she took care of the children. Marcia would do some aerobic dancing, calisthenics at home and play tennis with a girlfriend one evening a week.

Three: Rather than criticizing objectionable behavior, suggest a new approach. Allan and Marcia had a disagreement about a more sensitive issue, which had been the subject of a problem-solving session. Marcia felt that Allan was too critical of the children regarding cleanliness of their room; Allan felt that Marcia was too lenient. The couple generated these potential solutions in their problem-solving session.

Potential solutions	Degree of desirability	
	ALLAN	MARCIA
Allan stops yelling at the kids when their room is messy	5	10
Marcia stops ignoring the kids' messy room	10	5
Allan stops denying privileges when the room is untidy	1	10
Marcia stops allowing the kids to go out even though their room has not been cleaned up	10	5

This type of solution is a poor basis for negotiation because each partner requested that the other stop doing something irritating. A "stop-that" approach can destroy the potential for active change and can discourage the partner being criticized.

Keeping the reciprocity premise in mind, Allan and Marcia continued their discussion and came up with the following compromise after an open discussion with the children. Both would praise the children when their room was tidy. If the children's room was not cleaned up every day, Marcia agreed that the children should forfeit a portion of their allowance, and that three misdemeanors would mean no television. The children liked the plan and agreed to give it a try.

Four: Test negotiated agreements over a limited time period. Many couples come up with original, promising suggestions for compromise in their initial negotiation sessions, but find after a week that the solution they adopted so enthusiastically isn't working as well as they had hoped.

Testing an agreement for a limited period of time will help reduce the risk of failure. During the allotted time, both partners agree to do their best to respect the agreement; once the time is up, they discuss the success of the arrangement and the feasibility of its survival. Every agreement should be tentative until put to a practical test.

Allan and Marcia's agreement on physical exercise ran into some unexpected snags when Allan was forced to change his working hours. The contract on the children's bedroom was temporarily suspended by unanimous consent when one of the kids caught pneumonia and was housebound for two months. Both snags required some rearrangement of Allan and Marcia's original compromises.

Five: Define the terms of the compromise precisely. A negotiated agreement needs to be defined clearly and precisely or loopholes may cause it to fail. Allan and Marcia's original agreement about the children's room was this: Allan would offer more praise when the kids tidied their room and Marcia would be more strict about imposing punishment when they didn't. How much praise is "more"? How and when should Marcia impose punishment? Without these terms clearly defined, Allan could increase his praise while Marcia perceived the improvement to be inadequate. Similarly, Marcia punishing the kids more often might not be often enough for Allan. After further discussion with the children, the couple elaborated on their initial agreement and defined those points more specifically to avoid problems of interpretation.

Some disagreements are very difficult to settle through negotiation because essential facts are missing so partners cannot agree on the dimensions of their problem. For example, one couple did not have data on how many hours each was working, nor could they determine how important the woman's salary was without an accurate budget. Their negotiation ses-

132

sion on housework and work outside the home was postponed until these vital statistics were gathered. Many situations can be clarified if the partners agree to gather the necessary statistics and details before beginning negotiations: consumption of alcohol, cigarettes or fattening foods; time spent on work or leisure time spent together; how often they cleaned house; or income and expenditures.

Some couples find it helpful to end a negotiation session by writing down the agreement reached. Recording the decision ensures that, when the times comes to evaluate the success of the agreement, a lapse of memory will not cloud the discussion. In addition, while writing out their compromise, a couple may realize that some element of the plan has been expressed too vaguely. A written agreement also provides motivation: both partners may try harder to respect the plan if it is "official."

Other couples find that preparing a written contract is too formal, that unnecessary legalization "dehumanizes" their arrangement and takes too much time. Clearly, couples who have no difficulty remembering or respecting their verbal agreements need not waste time recording them. However, if disagreements arise – "That's not what we said we'd do" – a written contract can lessen the strain on the relationship.

Often, as soon as one partner notices that the other has failed to live up to their agreement, she/he immediately reneges. However, it is usually better to follow the contract until the time limit is reached. Then both partners can offer opinions on the strengths and weaknesses of the initial agreement, and the partner who first gave up can suggest modifications to the original agreement that would make it easier to follow.

Many differences between couples boil down to habit, and habits cannot be changed overnight. Allan's tendency to bark out at the children if their room was untidy and Marcia's tendency to forgive them lovingly for the same offense were both long-standing habits. When their first agreement about the children tidying their room had been in effect for about a week, Allan and Marcia reviewed their compromise. Allan felt he had upheld his end of the bargain "about half way," and Marcia was equally ambivalent about her own progress. They felt discouraged.

Many couples, at this point, are tempted to say to heck with negotiation. But anyone who has negotiated a satisfactory agreement and succeeded in following even half the agreed plan during the first week is doing very well. Marcia and Allan came to see that only through practice and sustained effort does compromise lead to lasting change: Allan tried to yell one less time and to offer praise one more time in the second week. Marcia tried to give in one less time and to put her foot down one more time.

Alice and Greg ran into problems similar to those of Allan and Marcia. Since Alice had started to work full-time, her cigarette smoking had increased to two packs a day. Both partners wanted a child and had been hoping that Alice would get pregnant within the year. Greg, a nonsmoker, sincerely wanted Alice to give up cigarettes before she became pregnant.

The couple had negotiated an agreement whereby Alice would quit smoking immediately and completely. Their negotiation session had ended on a very positive note, but their satisfaction with their arrangement lasted a mere three days. Alice stuck to the plan until the third evening, when Greg lashed out at her, "You've been eating like a pig since you stopped smoking, and you explode at the drop of a pin." Alice broke down in tears and within half an hour she had gone out to buy a pack of cigarettes, much to Greg's chagrin.

How could Alice and Greg have avoided their frustration? One strong shortcoming of their agreement was that it required effort only on Alice's part. Although both partners stood to profit if Alice stopped smoking – they had agreed to go on a vacation together once Alice had been off cigarettes for a month – the plan required nothing from Greg. True, cigarettes were Alice's problem, but a solution that demands input from both partners has a much greater chance of success. Greg and

Alice rehashed the three days that culminated in the fight and modified their agreement:

ALICE: I will quit smoking, starting right now. To keep my mind off cigarettes I will try to remain active doing repairs around the house and exercising. During the first month I will probably gain weight, but I won't restrict my eating; one problem at a time.

GREG: I will help Alice stop smoking by encouraging her efforts. I will emphasize the positive side of what she is doing; I will not mention what or how much she eats; and if she gets angry I will try to show understanding rather than irritation.

Their second attempt worked: Alice did gain eight pounds, but lost the weight the following summer. She was more irritable during the first ten days of her abstinence, but Greg found new ways to make her laugh and, according to Alice, "He kept me so busy doing things that I often forgot completely about cigarettes."

Irreconcilable Differences

Not all differences are negotiable. Any good partnership must balance respect for each individual's preferences, compromise and demands for change. But clearly, the success of any intimate relationship depends on compatibility. Partners who must constantly negotiate compromises on five or more vital issues will be under more pressure than partners who need to negotiate on only one or two.

In addition, partners' preferences may be reconcilable or irreconcilable. If she prefers to live in the Yukon wilderness and he in downtown Toronto, the complete satisfaction of one partner's preference would leave the other miserable, and any compromise would mean enormous losses for both partners.

It is not only the number of compromises required that will determine the overall happiness partners derive from their relationship. The amount of pleasure or satisfaction derived from each positive area is also important. If each partner derives enormous satisfaction from communication, mutual feelings of respect, support, sharing of responsibilities, time together with their children or working on common projects, then the losses resulting from accepting a somewhat unfavorable solution will seem small and easy to accept. However, a couple that has not developed or maintains a variety of mutual sources of satisfaction is at greater risk: both partners will simply feel that too much will be lost by any compromise.

For the reciprocity principle to work, both partners must be experiencing a variety of pluses in the relationship. Then each partner can intuitively sense the wisdom of compromise for the sake of the relationship. It is not easy for a partner who is not experiencing satisfaction in a relationship to accept the virtues of negotiation in good faith. So what should partners do when they are blocked by mutual mistrust? In Chapter Twelve, we will discuss deciding when and how to separate.

Reward and Punishment in Couple Negotiation

Proponents of the use of reward and punishment argue that, while most couples are fairly successful at reaching a workable agreement, many fail at putting it into action. Reward and punishment techniques work well in training children, so why not adults, too?

Greg and Alice, for example, could have included the following in their arrangement: Alice would receive five dollars each day she did not smoke but would have to do all the housework on days when she had a cigarette. Alice would reward Greg with a gourmet home-cooked meal at the end of each week during which he had upheld his side of the bargain, but he would have to do all the cooking any day he criticized Alice's eating habits or edginess.

Marcia and Allan's program to improve their skills as parents could have included these provisions for reward and punishment: Marcia would sleep in on the Sunday morning of every week she respected her contract but would have to take out the garbage for a week if she reneged. Allan would be allowed to watch football all Saturday afternoon if he respected his side of the bargain but would have to wash the dishes each night he yelled at the kids.

Whether incentive-deterrent bargaining actually helps distressed couples improve their relationship is not known, but it can create many new problems for couples. This type of arrangement is complicated to design and often difficult to put into operation. Secondly, many couples find the notion of introducing incentives and deterrents into their relationship distasteful. Thirdly, the rewards and punishments can generate new grounds for disagreements: "Your reward is greater than mine" or "My punishment is more drastic than yours." Finally, partners may disagree over whether a reward or punishment was deserved or administered fairly.

Rewards and punishments should only be part of marital negotiation conducted under the supervision of a trained professional. Indeed, partners who find they have great difficulty in implementing mutually accepted agreements would do well to consider consulting a marital specialist. (See Chapter Thirteen.)

Avoid Negotiation About Love and Sex
Negotiation and compromise are suitable for solving many problems that arise in a relationship, but these techniques are best left at the bedroom door. Negotiation requires a formal coolness, objectivity and effective problem-solving techniques; sharing of sensual pleasure is dependent upon spontaneity, passion and playfulness in a relaxed atmosphere. Expression of love and affection also demands sincerity: a partner needs to feel that a caress or compliment has been offered with genuine tenderness, not as part of a negotiated bargain.

8

How to Fight Constructively

Our culture has created many irrational beliefs about feeling and expressing anger. As a result, most people are poorly equipped behaviorally and emotionally to deal with anger. There are about as many "doves,"[6] couples who suffer from a fear of fighting, as there are "hawks," couples who fight too much with little positive gain. Unfortunately, our society offers few models for avoiding these two extreme ways of coping with anger; therefore, few couples know how to fight constructively.

Couples Who Never Fight: "Doves"
Betty and Jim (introduced in Chapter Three) felt increasingly bored with their relationship. Their couple checkup revealed that they rarely listened to each other and that Betty, in particular, rarely expressed her feelings. The checkup also disclosed that in all five years of their relationship, Betty and Jim had never had a fight, a fact each partner reported with pride. Jim later admitted he had been having occasional sexual relations with women he met at the department store where he worked. Betty responded that she had not made a scene when Jim told her this.

Here's how the couple discussed their problem:

JIM (sounding guilty): It never seemed to bother you much when I came in late Thursday nights.

BETTY (voice firm, but looking sad): Well, I always have too much work to do at the university. I used the occasions to get caught up a bit.

JIM (*sounding surprised and unsure of himself*): Other women would have been jealous.

BETTY (*defensively and a little sharply*): I'm not other women. What you do with your Thursday nights is your business.

It was not easy to discover what either partner was really thinking or feeling. It was only after several meetings that Betty talked about her parents' marriage. She revealed that her father had taken many lovers and that her mother was a "homebody and housewife," who used to frequently castigate her husband for his flings. Her father would not respond unless he was drinking. Then he would not only defend himself verbally by accusing his wife of being "frigid," but he would also resort to physical violence.

Much as she disapproved of her father, Betty vowed she would never become like her mother. She wanted above all never to be dependent, jealous or verbally abusive. Jim's affairs hurt her deeply and she worried that they resulted from some inadequacy in their relationship. But like many non-fighters, or "doves," she didn't want to rock the boat so she never voiced her anger and pain.

Jim did not hide his extramarital activities from Betty, claiming it had been their agreement to tell the other if either took a lover. He felt jealous of Betty's research at the university, which often kept her out late at night and away from him on weekends. However, he had never complained about her absence, because in his words: "She deserved her work and had so much pressure on the job that I did not want to add one more demand."

These doves faced many problems. Both had concerns about their partner and the relationship, but neither voiced them. As a result, they had achieved peace at a very high price. Their relationship, both agreed, had become extremely predictable and boring. They were having fewer sexual contacts and seldom with mutual satisfaction. Neither found their time together fulfilling. It was only a matter of months before Jim's flings would land him in a more satisfying relationship and he would leave Betty. It was this awareness that caused Betty to insist that they attend a couple-survival course.

Learning straightforward communication (as outlined in Chapter Three) went a long way to enrich their relationship, but it was not enough to deal with every important issue. Before presenting the steps that Betty and Jim followed to learn to fight fairly, we will look at a couple of "hawks" to get the whole picture.

Couples Who Fight Too Much, but Ineffectively: "Hawks"

Susan and Conrad had many explosive fights; but this last alteration was different. For the first time it ended with Susan throwing china. Conrad's face was cut badly, and he had retaliated with slaps that left Susan with a black eye. Friends suggested they seek help before something more serious happened.

Here is a typical exchange:

SUSAN (loudly): Why didn't you tell me you expected me to pick up the kids after school? They waited in the cold for an hour before the principal called me at work.

CONRAD (raising his voice): Don't yell at me. Don't you remember we had agreed you would pick them up yesterday?

SUSAN: But not the first Wednesday of the month. I always have a committee meeting then. You never listen! You're always thinking of your job, never of mine!

CONRAD: You're the one who told me just last night you wished I'd get a promotion. You're just like all career women. You want me to take over the child-rearing while you become vice-president!

SUSAN: Okay, if you insist, I'll quit my job, but we'll never make it on your salary.

This type of fight occurred daily; only the insults or timing would change. Sometimes they fought in front of their two kids, other times alone. Money, child-rearing, in-laws and how to spend their spare time were frequent triggers; but, after all the yelling and screaming, both partners would feel as frustrated as at the outset of the fight.

Anger Is Healthy

Few couples know how to deal with their aggression, and they avoid the extreme dovelike behavior of Jim and Betty or the overly hawklike stance of Susan and Conrad. But why would anyone want to learn how to fight? Shouldn't we simply choose our partner wisely and solve all our problems so that aggression and frustration are unnecessary? Certainly, compatibility will reduce frustration and other survival skills will take care of the rest. But anger between partners is inevitable and it can, when channeled properly, be a very constructive force.

Anger is a natural emotional and behavioral response to frustration. Everyone feels anger when a desire or a goal is denied, although the type of angry feelings or thoughts varies. And how that anger is expressed is equally variable.

Myths About Fighting

Our culture encourages some irrational notions about anger between intimates. Here are five accepted myths:

Myth One: Love and wise selection of a partner will eliminate all need for anger and fighting. Our parents, our friends and the media often suggest that, in the ideal relationship, people never get angry. This is a destructive notion because, while people may well share many beliefs, feelings and behaviors, they are bound to have differences. In fact, conflict may be a more frequent event in a couple's day than feelings of love. Couples have countless little decisions to make: when to get up, how to make love, when to tidy up. It is only natural that partners do not see eye to eye on everything, and that they become frustrated because each partner cannot always have his/her way.

For example, Jim likes to sleep in and cuddle in bed; Betty prefers to get up early. If Betty always went along with Jim's wishes she would always have her own wishes frustrated, just as Jim's desires would continually be denied if he always gave in to Betty's preferences.

Myth Two: If you feel angry with your partner, it is better not to express your frustration. Nothing positive can come from fighting. This damaging idea leads couples to attempt many ineffective strategies, such as keeping all gripes bottled up inside until an apparently trivial incident brings on extreme behavior such as physical violence or an unexpected petition for divorce. The dove style adopted by Jim and Betty in their need for peace at any price led to a steady accumulation of frustration, alienation and boredom.

While a lot of damage is done through destructive or inefficient fighting between partners, just as much harm is done between doves determined to suppress their anger and their natural urge to fight.

Myth Three: Only people with immature personalities or people from troubled childhoods get angry often and express their anger verbally. To identify and express anger effectively requires a mature personality and a healthy relationship. Most couples who show no outward signs of anger are either irrationally afraid of their own or their partner's aggressive feelings or are so uninvolved in the relationship that they don't care.

Certainly some people with disturbed personalities or troubled backgrounds declare verbal and physical war on their partners with little provocation. But just because some people express their aggressive feelings ineffectively does not mean that all aggression is unwarranted and ineffective.

Myth Four: Frequent fights between partners indicate high dissatisfaction with the relationship and/or imminent separation. It is not whether a couple fights, but how, why and when they fight that determines whether the relationship is in trouble. Fighting can improve awareness of self and others, release tension within and between individuals and open the way to more honest and effective communications and problem-solving. It can also speed effective compromise, equally distribute power and control, enable each partner to establish her/his own distance and individuality and trigger renewed appreciation of the other's goals and feelings.

Myth Five: If I get angry, my partner will see my negative side and reject me. This fear depends upon how you express your anger, what you get angry about and what your partner is like.

The third component, the nature of your partner, is by far the most complex. Many couples include one partner who wants to learn how to fight fairly and another who is a diehard dove. One partner would like to express frustration constructively, but is afraid that his/her partner will: "hit me," "cry," "walk out" or "hate me."

Too many of us drastically overestimate the negative impact of our anger on our partner. Betty found that Jim respected and desired her more once she was able to fight constructively. She had always avoided fighting because she interpreted fighting as a barrage of insults, physical assaults and threats that signaled the deterioration of a relationship. She had never seen the constructive side of fighting.

To fight constructively and fairly couples must recognize when, where and about what to fight. Then they must learn what to do during the heat of the battle to allow for a clean fight.

Fair Fighting: When, Where and Over What

Rule One: Know when and where to fight. Making love and making war, if they are to produce the desired results, are best conducted at certain times and in certain places. (Couples who rarely fight can often profit from scheduling one fight a week.) Doves tend to have too many restrictions on time and place. For example, showing affection or lovemaking is restricted: "Not in front of the kids," "Not in front of the guests," "Not in front of your mother," "Not when I get up," "Not if you want to make love tonight," "Not while we're eating," "Not while this program is on," "Not after the day I've had."

Couples who fight too often or too destructively tend to disregard time and place. The objective of fair and constructive fighting is to communicate what happened or what made us feel hurt, angry or frustrated. If we really want our partner to hear our message we must choose a time when we are both under control, so that the message will be comprehensible – able to be received and understood.

Couples who fight too often or too destructively should determine the right time to fight. It is usually better to avoid fights when one or both partners have just come home from work; in the middle of the night, when one wants to go to sleep; while either is driving (fatal accidents are two to three times higher among couples in crisis); and while either is drinking, if liquor leads one or both to be more stubborn or more aggressive.

"Hawks" should ask themselves: "If I attack now, will it really make a difference?" "Is there a better time to fight?" "Is there a better way to deal with my frustration?" Some overly aggressive partners have found that physical exercise, manual labor or putting one's thoughts and feelings down on paper can reduce frustration better than verbally expressing every feeling of anger.

Rule Two: Know what you're angry about before starting a fight. The two major goals of fighting are to reduce frustration and to bring about changes for the better. Therefore, from the outset, both partners must know what the fight is about.

Instead of instigating a discussion with your partner, start a conversation with yourself. What am I angry about? Is it something my partner did, said, thought? Is it something my partner feel? The way she/he looks? My partner did something that bugs me: is it what he/she did or is it the reason for doing it that makes me so angry? Do I really know my partner's motives and intentions, or should I ask questions instead of attacking?

If I get angry, will it make a difference? Can my partner really make a change, or is it outside her/his control? Do I want to express my anger to improve the situation or simply to punish my partner? Instead of hurting him/her, is there something I can do that will make me feel better and improve our situation? I'm angry about many things, but which gripe shall I bring up now? Is it something that can be remedied? If I bring it up, am I willing to stay with it? Perhaps I'm angry with my spouse for certain reasons, but to what extent am I responsible for the problems? If I bring a complaint out in the open, can I think of something that I or my partner can do to improve the situation?

Doves find these questions easier to answer than hawks, who, confronted with such a long list, frequently respond: "I never could analyze my motives. I'm already out of control when I realize I'm angry." However, many hawks can learn to stand back and analyze fights, to recognize the warning signs. They could have bought time instead of rushing into battle. When couples take brief notes about their fights, they realize there are some high-risk times for the outbreak of warfare. The next time one of these moments arrives – "tomorrow night when the kids haven't gone to bed on time" or "tomorrow when he doesn't pick up his laundry" or "next time we try to make love" – each partner should be prepared by the answers to the questions cited above.

What if a couple tries to answer the questions but cannot? What if they realize that, if they fight, it will not reduce their frustration or improve their relationship? Many find that a postponement works wonders for improving the quality of fights. For example, one partner might say: "I'm really pissed off at you but I'm not sure why, so can we fight later?" or "I'm so angry now I'd better calm down and go for a jog." If your partner starts a fight with an opening line that, in the past, has invariably led to a dirty fight, try: "What you said ticks me off, but I'll take a raincheck on fighting about it, okay?" Then get up and leave the room.

Rule Three: Fight about problems that can be solved. If you want to fight to release frustration or to change a painful situation, always tackle a problem you or your partner can do something about.

Susan and Conrad fought daily. When they wrote down what they fought about, an interesting picture emerged: they locked horns on concrete problems they could actually do something about only 50 per cent of the time. Once Susan and Conrad had each gathered their "fight log" for the week, they answered two questions about each fight. Was it a past or a current problem? Was it about an open or a dead issue? Fights about "the job he/she shouldn't have left," "the holiday we missed," "the time she/he hurt my mother," "the time she/he insulted my friend" only encourage accusations and counter-accusations.

For example:

CONRAD: We should never have sold our old country cottage.
SUSAN: It was your idea.
CONRAD: Yeah, but you're the one who called the real-estate agent.
SUSAN: Because you whined and complained so much.

Of course, it is not easy to forget previous hurts. However, past history only becomes productive material for a fight if the consequences of the past can be altered in the present. Conrad and Susan were asked, "What have you learned from having sold the house in the country? What did you lose by selling it?" Both agreed that it was a place where daily employment was left behind, where they sat around, read together, walked together and played with the kids. Both missed these activities, which had almost totally stopped since the cottage was sold two years earlier. The problem that still occurred was their frustration at rarely spending time together. Therefore this, rather than the cottage, was a constructive thing to fight about.

Not only can memories of past events trigger anger toward our mate, but a partner can become angered by a characteristic or state of affairs that is irreversible: "If only you were taller"; "If only you were younger"; "If only you weren't going bald"; "If only you had bigger breasts"; "We would be better off if you hadn't quit school"; "Why weren't you a doctor instead of a carpenter?" "If only you could give me more children." Before voicing a complaint, partners should ask themselves: "Is this a dead-end issue, or can I or my partner do something about the source of my frustration?"

There are many disadvantages to voicing dead-end gripes: for example, a drop in your partner's self-esteem and happiness or a decline in motivation to improve remediable behavior. As well, dead-end gripes can be contagious: if one partner expresses this type of complaint, the other will likely respond in kind.

Rule Four: Fight about one gripe at a time. Many car owners, when taking their car for a tuneup, hand over the keys and leave the service manager with a long, disorganized list of repair jobs to be done. Perhaps the wipers don't work, the radio antenna is broken, the brakes jam and the oil level drops unpredictably. The mechanic may be able to give only two hours of work to it the next morning, and a full day a week later. Because car owners have not specified which jobs they want handled first, they may well find, when they pick up the car, that only the minor repairs have been done; the car will remain out of commission until the major problems are fixed.

Ineffective fighting can be just as frustrating and inefficient. By not ranking complaints in order of priority, and by voicing several gripes at one time, couples only compound their difficulties.

In Conrad and Susan's fight early in this chapter, each brought up at least three gripes. Susan's were: fetch the kids; think of my career; make more money. Conrad's were: respect our original schedule; stop nagging me about getting ahead; stop trying to get me to spend more time with the kids. For them to feel less frustrated, the couple first had to learn not to fight over all their complaints in one fight session, but to tackle one gripe at a time.

Rule Five: Fight about the real problem, not the side issues. Many people have fights that appear to be about one subject but are actually about something else. Without realizing it, Karen (described in Chapter Five) would often become angry with Rubin when she thought he would initiate sex. But their fights were never about sex; work, money or the house would be the real issue. When Dave initiated fights with Jeanne over the gifts she gave her mother (Chapter Six), what really made him angry was that Jeanne brought no revenue into the household.

The danger of not pinpointing the true source of frustration is that the criticized partner can hardly be expected to shape up without really knowing what or how to change.

Fair Fighting

Once couples have learned when, how, and over what to fight, they are more than halfway to becoming fair fighters. Next, they must master the steps to apply during the heat of the battle.

Rule One: Use "I" and take responsibility for what you think and feel. We saw, in Chapter Three, that communication can be greatly enhanced if an individual expresses him/herself in the first person: "I wish you would take out the garbage" instead of "Take out the garbage"; or "I was disappointed you didn't come home on time for supper" instead of "Why didn't you come home for supper?"

When an angry partner says "I" instead of "We" or "One" or "Our family," he/she assumes an adult and responsible place in the relationship. Partners who shield themselves behind general or collective labels suppress their own identity; they also put the receiver of their complaint at an unfair disadvantage. How can she/he develop a constructive response to the anger of people in general? If both partners use "I" to express their thoughts and feelings, they will keep to the real issues and manageable problems.

Rule Two: Call your partner by name. Do not use insulting labels or impersonal pronouns. Often in the heat of battle we're tempted to insult our partners with names we think might be hurtful. Although a desire to strike out when we're abused or frustrated is natural, name calling is not a very effective way to retaliate.

Insults only enrage our partner, and name calling begets name calling. Hawks often specialize in highly original but injurious insults.

Doves, on the other hand, resort to generalizations and impersonal statements. When they try to air their grievances it is often not clear exactly who the gripe is about or what the real problem is.

For example, when Jim and Betty discussed the fact that Jim regularly slept with other women on Thursday nights, they had this exchange:

JIM: They say that people who practise open marriage stay together longer because they never get bored with each other.

BETTY: You never know when a person might discover that the grass is greener on the other side.

JIM: Why would anyone leave a nest where he can have his cake and eat it too?

After a few practice sessions, Jim and Betty were able to reject the impersonal pronouns and to discuss their own feelings about their own marriage, not marriages in general:

BETTY *(voice shaking)*: I'm worried that you'll fall in love with another woman and divorce me.

JIM *(sounding reassuring)*: I really don't think there's a risk that I'll find anyone who could replace you.

BETTY *(voice increasingly agitated)*: That's the way it always starts. You sleep with someone Thursday night. For now you say it's a casual relationship, but I'm worried that whoever she is might eventually replace me.

JIM *(defensively)*: I'm glad you finally got around to telling me this. I thought you didn't care.

Jim and Betty are now on the right track. By using "I" and "you," each has taken responsibility for identifying and disclosing his/her own feelings. This is crucial if the couple wants their fight to bring about a positive change in behavior.

Rule Three: Verify what your partner's feelings and intentions are. Do not try to be a mind reader. Betty and Jim always assumed they knew the other's feelings and intentions. In reality, though, both were misreading the other's mind so they never dealt with the real issues:

JIM (*mind reading Betty's feelings*): Because you kept on working at the office and never said anything, I figured my night out wasn't bothering you.

BETTY (*mind reading Jim's intentions*): I figured you would only be sleeping around if you were looking for a new woman to replace me.

It is tempting to assume that we know why our partner thinks, feels and acts in certain ways. It is also easy to assume that our partner knows why we act, think and feel the way we do. But mind reading leads to false interpretations of acts and emotions. During an exchange between angry or hurt partners, each tends to become less rational. Emotions then come to influence how reality is perceived. The angrier we get, the less we are able to diagnose our partner's intentions accurately or objectively. One of the simplest ways to avoid jumping to erroneous conclusions is to verify information and not to assume anything. Jim and Betty rapidly learned this skill:

JIM: When you didn't say anything about my late Thursday nights, I assumed you didn't mind. How did you react?

BETTY (*taking a risk made easier by Jim's open question*): Now I realize it made me angry and jealous, and I'm worried that I would lose you.

Doves such as Jim and Betty often find it relatively easy to learn this skill. Because they are more accustomed to keeping a lid on their emotions, they can retain some objectivity. Hawks such as Conrad and Susan, more used to fights of blood-boiling intensity, have trouble seeing and thinking clearly, and tend to mind read:

SUSAN (*attributing motives to Conrad*): I bet you didn't pick the kids up because you wanted to get back at me for not accepting your invitation for sex last night.

CONRAD *(sarcastically)*: My dear, you were the one who wanted to make love last night. I was too tired. I didn't pick them up because I assumed you would prefer to be there Wednesday. That's the day your old body-building friend coaches in the gym next door.

Susan assumed Conrad was motivated by sexual frustration, which in turn provoked his anger and reprisal. Conrad assumed Susan preferred to pick up the kids on Wednesday so she could flirt with an old flame. Although they were supposedly attempting to solve a problem, their mind reading distracted them from it. As a result, their fight was not constructive.

Rule Four: Become more objective about your own fight style by tape-recording your fights and by fighting in front of neutral observers. Conrad and Susan began to tape-record their fight sessions at home. Afterwards each took turns alone listening to the tape to analyze their own way of talking and interacting. (Generally, it is far more productive to look for ways to improve our own communication skills than to assess those of our partner.)

After listening to several of their taped fights, Conrad and Susan recognized how much mind reading each had been doing, and how often it led to unfounded conclusions. They also noticed how often the fights would turn especially vicious after one partner ascribed dark or secret motives to the other's actions. In addition, they realized that their most bitter fights were usually not about "who did what to whom" but about "why the other did what she/he did." By reducing their mind reading, and by attempting verification, Conrad and Susan brought about a noticeable improvement in the outcomes of their fights. Now, instead of ending in stalemate, fights actually end with each partner making suggestions for change.

At times, a fight in front of a third party can help to increase a partner's objectivity, provided the observer does not take sides.

Rule Five: Make your complaints specific. One of the benefits of a good fight is that it can allow couples to discover what is really on each other's minds. In the heat of the battle, discretion is thrown to the wind and statements may be made that are usually not risked. We may even discover facets of ourselves we did not know existed. Such a voyage of self-discovery can be especially valuable for doves like Betty and Jim. After they became more accustomed to voicing what was really on their minds, the following exchange took place:

JIM: If you weren't so cool in bed, I wouldn't be so inclined to go out cruising Thursday nights.
BETTY: If you weren't so self-centered in bed, I wouldn't be so "cool," as you put it.

This is good, for two people who used to be non-fighters. Betty and Jim have started to talk about one of the real issues. They are ready to admit that all is not perfect in their sex life. Now they have a much better chance of improving it than they did when they used to claim all was well in the bedroom.

Yet Betty and Jim needed to take their last exchange one step further if they hoped for improvement. Each had used unspecific words like "cool" and "self-centered," when describing the other's sexual behavior, leaving too much leeway for mind reading. If, after the fight is over, Betty resolves to become "less cool" and Jim "less self-centered," how could they achieve these goals?

One of the best strategies could be to adopt the X-Y-Z approach;[2] XYZ represents the way to describe a complaint by behavior, situation and impact, to give the whole picture. When your partner next does something that irritates you, it could be described according to XYZ like this: "When you do X (behavior) in Y (situations) I feel Z (impact)." Jim's complaint would thus become: "If you don't speak a word (X-behavior) when we are in bed (Y-situation) I feel lost and confused about what turns you on or off (Z-impact)." And Betty's criticism would become: "When you have your orgasm early (X-behavior), when we're making love (Y-situation), I feel sexually frustrated and angry (Z-impact)."

Hawk couples like Conrad and Susan could also benefit greatly from the X-Y-Z method of voicing gripes. One of their frequent round robins concerned their children. Their two boys, aged seven and nine, were beginning to have discipline problems at school. At home, they rarely obeyed their parents' rules on bedtime and homework. Although the boys were obviously bright and otherwise endearing, their disobedience undermined Susan and Conrad's authority.

SUSAN: I've told you time and time again you've got to stop being such a pushover with the kids at bedtime.

CONRAD: Me, a pushover? You're the original easy make when it comes to giving them their allowance.

Clearly this way of exchanging complaints will not resolve the couple's problems, but will only lead to heated tempers and frustration. This is how the couple could have relayed their complaints using the X-Y-Z method:

SUSAN: When it's time for the boys to go to bed (Y-situation), you let them stay up too long (X-behavior) and I feel you shirk your responsibility as a parent (Z-impact).

CONRAD: When the boys ask for money (Y-situation), you often give them too much (X-behavior) and I feel you're spoiling them (Z-impact).

Rule Six: Follow your complaint with a request for a positive change. In all the arguments between Betty and Jim, and between Susan and Conrad, each partner requested that the other stop doing something that irritated them. By ending the fight there, both couples failed to get all the potential from their exchanges. After specifying what they didn't like, they should have specified what would have pleased them. The chances, then, of each couple forging positive and lasting improvements in their relationship would have increased.

Betty, for example, could have said: "When we make love (Y-situation), if you would hold off your orgasm for a while longer (X-positive behavioral change), I would feel more pleasure (Z-positive impact)." Jim could have responded: "If, while we're in bed (Y-situation), you would tell me what excites you (X-new positive behavior), I would feel more at ease and be able to please you better (Z-new positive impact)."

Conrad could have said: "If, when the kids ask for money (Y-situation), you would only give them the agreed upon weekly allowance (X-new positive behavior), I think it would teach them to value money better (Z-new positive consequence)." And Susan could have responded: "At bedtime (Y-situation), if you would remind the boys once, then send them to bed within five minutes (X-new behavior), I think it would be more consistent with what they need (Z-new positive consequence)."

All couples must remember to finish a complaint with a concrete proposal for new positive behavior. If we only ask our partner to stop doing something that upsets us, she/he may simply suppress the response for a while. But the suppression is likely to be temporary, at best. Change will be easier and more lasting if, instead of punishing old behaviors, partners concentrate on adopting new ones. Requesting positive new behaviors is the best strategy for keeping fights fair, realistic and productive. Fighting can teach your partner things about you that can be very valuable; however, some complaints are simply the product of momentary anger. Once tempers have cooled, couples realize that they do not stand up to the self-exploration questions described on pp. 144-145. One of the best tests of whether you have a dead-end gripe is to ask yourself: "Can I make a new positive request in the 'X-Y-Z' form?" If the answer is no, then you would probably be better off finding another way to reduce your anger.

Rule Seven: Recognize your own part in the problem and in the solution. Don't play the blaming game. When couples are asked what is responsible for the current hostility, frustration or sexual dysfunction in their relationship, they invariably answer that one person is mainly to blame. In dove marriages, one or both partners claim it's their fault.

For example, Betty said: "It's my fault, because I'm too cold and introverted." In hawk relationships in which both partners are used to venting their frustration through aggression, each blames the other, absolving themselves of all guilt. Moreover, fighting hawks will often try to cajole witnesses (therapists, friends, relatives, children or innocent bystanders) to join the only right side of the argument, namely their own.

But there is rarely just one person at fault in an unhappy or destructive relationship. One of the most convincing ways to demonstrate this is to watch videotapes of a couple's fight patterns. Couples living together become involved in a complex pattern of interaction – a dance of sorts – in which they "teach" each other how to behave. Her yawn, for example, is followed by his frown, which causes him to feel defensive and attack her verbally, which then leads her to think, irrationally, that he doesn't like her looks. In fact, he is feeling frustrated with his job; but because both partners are merely performing a set of maneuvers, neither is conveying fears, doubts and frustrations. Both are equally to blame for the poor communication.

Observers of fight patterns have to exercise a great degree of mental agility to interpret the effect one partner's actions or gestures has upon the other. Couples, too, must develop this agility if they are to observe and comprehend their partner's actions, while remaining aware of their own behavior. Partners must ask themselves: "Can I pinpoint what it is she/he does that upsets me? Can I specify what she/he can do to change?" They must also ask: "What part do I play in triggering the problems? What can I do to improve our relationship?" When partners, especially hawks, admit responsibility for a problem out loud, tempers are defused and constructive solutions can be put into place.

For example, a more constructive ending to the fight between Susan and Conrad over who picks up the children from school went like this.

CONRAD: Our schedules are confusing. Now I remember you said you wanted me to pick up the kids, but your committee meeting always used to be on Monday nights.
SUSAN: You're right, and last week it changed to Thursday. I remember telling you this morning the meeting was today, but perhaps you didn't hear me because one of the kids was yelling. How would it be if just before we leave each morning we remind each other whose turn it is to pick up the children.

9

Fights: Reducing the Risks, Making Up, and Keeping Score

Violence between partners and between parents, especially fathers, and their offspring is on the increase in western cultures. A person is much more likely to die at the hand of a spouse or parent than at the hand of a stranger. In Chapter Eight, we saw that name calling is an unproductive way to express anger. Name calling should be prohibited, as should yelling, throwing things, hitting, slapping, rape and bondage, because they increase the amount of anger felt and expressed. Murder or physical injury of spouses is rarely the product of one incident; it usually begins with a reasonable expression of anger and then escalates to name calling, to threats and finally to physical abuse.

It's not the names themselves that are so potentially damaging, for while some couples stop at verbal abuse, others will use it as a stepping stone to threats and then to physical abuse.

In violent arguments, both partners obstinately want to win. Each wants the other to change his/her behavior and admit: "You're right. I give in." As we saw in Chapter Eight, it is natural and, indeed, constructive to attempt to influence your partner to change; but much depends on how you go about it. Couples who control each other in their fights mainly through punishing or name calling can become addicted to the same old fight routine. They become locked in a pattern they cannot escape.

The fights between Hank, a truck driver, and Sheila, a nursing assistant, usually included bouts of yelling and name calling. A fight took place every Friday night after both partners had spent a long, hard week at work; their four-year-old daughter and six-year-old son were in bed. One fight was different: Sheila ended up black and blue in the hospital. After drinking no more than two beers each, the couple began to argue about mutual complaints: lack of money, the division of housework, how little time they spent together. Before long, the name calling began:

SHEILA *(yelling)*: You unfeeling bastard. You only think of your own needs. You never think I'd like a break, too.

HANK: If you call me a bastard one more time, I'll show you just what a bastard I can be.

SHEILA: Here you go again with your threats. I refuse to be afraid of you, my own sweet loser of a husband.

HANK *(quickly losing his temper as he recalls their earlier talk about his fear of being laid off in favor of a younger, stronger employee)*: You bitch, you're asking for it. Whose side are you on, anyway?

SHEILA *(feeling enraged by his insult and his veiled accusation that she isn't being supportive of him, yet not about to back down and lose the fight)*: I've been propping you up ever since you hurt your back and moped around here for a year on unemployment insurance.

(Hank sees red at this last insult. He rushes across the room and slaps Sheila.)

SHEILA *(equally enraged, and not about to give in)*: You cowardly bastard, hitting a woman.

(Hank is even more angered by Sheila's last insult and hits her repeatedly on the face and shoulders until she falls, unconscious.)

After the couple exchanged their first insults and name calling, Sheila said, "Here you go again." This expressed what both were feeling. Once locked into name calling, each knew the only way she/he could win the battle was to try out a new weapon. In this instance, Hank moved first and chose physical violence.

Reducing the Risks of Physical Violence

Couples rarely plot strategy in their fights; but both try desperately to win. With one's self-esteem and one's worth as a human being on the line, the stakes are high. Both partners may feel: "If I let this person who knows me so well and to whom I've given so much get away with calling me names, I'll be admitting I'm worthless." The partners will then both feel ready to do *anything* in the struggle to avoid the sense of personal annihilation.

Many couples say: "There's no harm in a little yelling, name calling and the occasional shoving or dish throwing. We know when to stop." But most couples who indulge in this behavior find themselves progressing from name calling and yelling to "sticks-and-stones" tactics. Sometimes, the spiral of aggression grows during several years, allowing the couple time to take preventive steps. Other couples, however, turn to physical violence with little warning, provoked by drunkenness, fatigue or excessive vulnerability. Frustration with events outside the home – job pressure or unemployment – can also trigger a violent outburst, as can injured pride when a partner's insult inflicts more damage than intended.

If you have noticed increasingly destructive aggression in your relationship – perhaps the insults are getting dirtier and more frequent or there has been an exchange of blows – follow the steps below.

What should you do if your partner beats you? Although many people prefer not to talk about this issue, one in every ten North American women is beaten by her partner.[7] Yet most women who are beaten regularly do not tell anyone about it. They are either afraid of their partner's retaliation, believe at some level that they deserve to be beaten, have nowhere to go or, if they leave their home, want to protect the man who is attacking them.

Battered women should seek emotional and physical protection from a competent third party. Some North American communities now have centers that can provide the battered woman (and her children, if necessary) with the emotional and physical shelter she needs. The names and addresses of these centers can be obtained from women's health centers, from your local YWCA or from the emergency number of your local police. However, due to budget cuts and chronic under-funding, these centers are too small to meet all the needs of their communities. Police, social workers, psychologists, psychiatrists, general practitioners and clergy can also provide valuable support and advice. With a competent consultant, the battered woman can define the problems she faces and choose the best solutions. Often, physical distance from her partner is the only effective way to guarantee that the physical abuse will stop. Once her life is no longer in danger, the woman can take steps to improve her relationship or to seek a constructive separation. Some battered women feel they cannot possibly leave their partners, even though the men may place the women's lives in constant danger.

Once you have identified the warning signs of violent behavior in your relationship, attempt to discuss the matter. However, choose your moment carefully. Do not broach the subject to express your aggression or frustration; request a ceasefire or de-escalation of battle. The object is to reduce the risk that one or both of you will start the fight that ends all fights.

Do not fight until you have learned to fight constructively, once you have reinforced the more positive aspects of your relationship. Do this through skillful listening (Chapter Three), through problem solving (Chapter Six), through love and affection (Chapter Four) and/or sensuality (Chapter Five). Hawk couples may reach a stage of aggression at which constructive fighting becomes impossible. These couples must work very hard to keep their fighting to a minimum until the positive features of their relationship are strong enough to withstand the venting of frustrations. They must first build a framework of respect and mutual regard; otherwise, arguments will degenerate into full-fledged battles.

Carefully learn to follow the "when, what and how" rules of constructive fighting described in Chapter Eight; as soon as you see that either of you is having difficulty following them, politely request a postponement of the fight until a more suitable time.

How and Why to Make Up After a Fight

One of the richest rewards of fair fighting is the experience of making up. Couples who know how to make up, and who are not afraid to do so, enjoy this phase: "It's the calm after the storm"; "I enjoy cuddling after we've made peace, because I can feel so lonely and distant from my partner during a fight"; "After we have spent time looking at the weaknesses in each other, it's wonderful to get back in touch with why we're together and why we like each other"; "Forgiving my spouse for an angry outburst or when my spouse forgives me reminds me of when I was a child. After I had been naughty and had been reprimanded, my parents would say: 'Okay, you've had your punishment. Now, let's get back to having fun.' I feel emotional, relieved and comforted."

Many couples are afraid of making up, because they equate it with forgiving and forgetting; but that doesn't have to be the case. Some fights are born of frustrations that cannot be resolved through anger. They can only be resolved if the partners calm down and spend a good deal of time discussing, listening, problem solving and negotiating. Other fights can only be resolved through improvements in the expression of love and sensuality. Occasionally, the behavior or actions that trigger fights can never be eradicated, and the offended partner either has to tolerate the discomfort or separate from her/his mate.

Ideally, fights should last from a few hours to almost a day. It is always best to make up rather than carry the fight over to the next day.

Remember, the objectives of constructive fighting are to reduce frustration and to increase the quality of a relationship. If partners are not willing to declare peace, these objectives will not be reached. Making peace requires that the couple act positively together and that they forget their differences, however temporarily. Most individuals stay in a relationship because it brings them more pleasure and less pain than other alternatives. Making up involves a reaffirmation of the pleasurable aspects of the partnership. Partners not willing or able to make up will affirm the negative aspects; if they outweigh the positive ones, partners are likely to ask themselves: "Is the relationship worth it?"

A fight, if kept within reasonable time limits, can have positive results: it can reduce tension; disclose bottled-up emotions; pinpoint problems; and re-establish the independent identity of both partners. If the partners make up soon after the fight, each can use the energy and information gained from the fight to make adjustments in the relationship. But if one or both partners sulks or refuses to communicate or "give in," the positive potential of the fight will not be realized.

Conrad and Susan were reluctant to make peace after their fights:

CONRAD: I don't like to make up because I feel I'm admitting that I was wrong or that I was a fool or that I was the only one to blame.

SUSAN: I won't make up because I refuse to pardon Conrad for his insults or for his deliberate efforts to hurt me. Besides, if I make up, I'm afraid he will believe that I did not mean what I said or think that all is forgotten, which is never the case.

Both seemed interested in the advantages of making up but remained somewhat skeptical, as neither had learned the techniques:

CONRAD: After a fight I usually go to sleep, and by morning I've forgotten the anger.

SUSAN: I'm the same way. If we don't speak to each other or see each other for a few hours, my anger will often lessen so that I don't feel like fighting anymore.

Making up involves words and deeds, saying peaceable things to each other and making kind or affectionate gestures, such as:

Words

1. "Can we make up now?"
2. "Shall we let our differences rest for a while?"
3. "I think we've got all the mileage out of this fight for today."
4. "I know we haven't solved all the problems you raised, but can we make up now?"
5. "I don't think we'll get anywhere if we keep on fighting. Can we discuss the problem tomorrow, and in the meantime . . .?"

Deeds

1. Pull out a white handkerchief and wave it.
2. Offer flowers.
3. Send a love note.
4. Hug or kiss.
5. Put on a record you know your partner enjoys.
6. Participate in a sport together.
7. Make love.

Conrad and Susan had to learn that making up does not have to mean forgetting all that was said during or learned from the fight. Instead, it can mean: "Let's stop fighting about our differences, and do something positive together so we can overcome them." Couples who possess fair-fighting and problem-solving skills can use their fights to sensitize each other to the "what" and "why" of a problem, so making up is easier. The restricted weapons of abuse and violence can be put away, as the partners knuckle down to the job of finding mutually acceptable solutions.

Why Fight? It's Too Complicated and Dangerous

Doves often say: "Oh, this is all too complicated. Wouldn't it be easier never to express aggression, given the potential for violence in all of us?"

Hawks see it another way: "My aggressive feelings are so strong and dangerous, I am more afraid of them than ever and of what they can do to my marriage. Wouldn't it be better to go cold turkey like an alcoholic and never let myself express anger?" Let us explore these understandable reactions.

Both doves and hawks will have to work hard to learn fair fighting. (Some will find it easier and safer to learn to fight fairly with the help of a competent professional.) Stifling aggression indefinitely or trying to go "cold turkey" will not resolve anything in the long run. Both doves and hawks may tell themselves it would be different or easier or better with another partner: "I won't change my ways, I'll change partners." However, if you do not express your anger, or if you are constantly angry at your partner, without the skills to deal with your antagonism, you will most likely experience the same problems with a new partner.

Most couples are neither hawks nor doves, but fall between the extremes. These partners do not need marital or individual therapy, but can learn the necessary skills of fair fighting from this book or from a couple-enrichment or couple-communication course. Either way, learning the skills takes time and energy – physical, intellectual and emotional energy. A relationship rich in diversity, trust and intimacy demands that both partners work hard and long on every aspect of it.

Many couples value a happy relationship above all else, yet invest much more energy and many more hours, days and years in their jobs, sports activities and accumulating wealth.

The average couple could learn how to fight fairly in fifty to two hundred hours: reading, discussing, practising exercises and perhaps attending a couple-survival course. If two hundred hours sounds like too much time, ask yourself the following questions:

1. How many full days is two hundred hours?
2. How many hours a week or year do I watch television?
3. How many hours a week or year do I spend taking other courses?
4. How much time do I spend on sports or other leisure activities?

5. How much time a week do my partner and I spend together in boring activities or fighting?

For many partners, the number of hours invested in such activities easily surpasses two hundred. Investing the same number of hours in learning how to fight fairly to build a harmonious relationship, one of the most important goals in life, is not unreasonable.

But do we really need to learn how to fight? Wouldn't it be better to find other ways to express, decrease or control aggression? In the long run, all couples benefit from mastering the skills of fair fighting; but many couples should first improve their listening, loving and problem-solving skills. Couples with good problem-solving skills or a satisfying sexual relationship feel frustrated less often and thus feel less need to fight. Therefore, developing the other couple-survival skills makes the need for expertise in fair fighting less urgent.

After a fight, the two most important skills to develop are learning from the fight and making up. It is much easier to learn from a fight if you already know how to express yourself and to listen. Similarly, it is simpler to make up if you can offer a variety of positive activities: lovemaking, for example, or the ability to share in leisure activities.

Fair fighting allows for self-exploration, permits a clear definition of how you differ from your partner, affirms your independent emotional identities, establishes distance, reduces the risk of taking peace for granted, removes tension and increases intimacy and sharing.

How Do Problem-Solving and Fair Fighting Differ?

At times, couples will unconsciously mix these activities; but most couples find it easier to keep fighting and problem-solving separate, because each has different objectives and gains.

The objectives of fighting are to air grievances, to express anger and to reduce frustration. The fair-fighting rules prevent destructive behavior but leave room for letting off steam: "I'm angry," "I'm hurt," "I feel let down," "I feel cheated." There is room, too, for tears, raised voices and dramatic

164

arguments to support feelings. But once the fight has achieved its purpose – venting frustration and heightening mutual awareness – problem-solving and negotiating should be put off for a while, unless the couple is in a crisis that demands a quick decision. For problem-solving is easier, more satisfying and achieves more effective results once the fight is over, when the feelings of frustration are under control and the head is clear enough to tackle problem-solving.

How to Evaluate Your Own Fight Patterns

Before two partners make the commitment to improve their fighting skills, they should first examine their present fight styles. This scoring system is quite simple and summarizes our discussion of fair fighting.

How to Evaluate Your Fight Patterns

Answer each of the following questions by circling yes or no and the + 1 or –1 below it.

	Yes	No
1. Do you believe that if you have chosen your partner well you never need to fight?	Yes –1	No + 1
2. Do you think that fighting is a natural and inevitable part of any intimate relationship?	Yes + 1	No –1
3. Do you believe that when you're angry, it is always better to keep the feeling inside?	Yes –1	No + 1
4. Do you think your partner is the one most responsible for the problems in your relationship?	Yes –1	No + 1
5. Do you and your partner fight at any time and in any place, instead of carefully choosing a time and place to do so?	Yes –1	No + 1
6. Do you pick a fight with your partner when he/she is obviously tired or grumpy, or after he/she has just arrived home from work?	Yes –1	No + 1

7. Do you air grievances soon after they occur instead of waiting for months to do so?

	Yes	No
	+1	-1

8. When you start a fight with your partner, do you usually know why you're angry?

	Yes	No
	+1	-1

9. Do you find that you and your partner have sudden angry outbursts with few, if any, warning signs?

	Yes	No
	-1	+1

10. Do you often criticize your partner about one thing when you're really angry about something else?

	Yes	No
	-1	+1

11. Do you usually fight about one issue at a time instead of voicing several complaints in the same fight?

	Yes	No
	+1	-1

12. Do you often criticize your partner for things she/he cannot change, such as physical size, race, color of skin or family background?

	Yes	No
	-1	+1

13. Do you and your partner often fight about problems that occurred months or years ago?

	Yes	No
	-1	+1

14. When you express anger or frustration with your partner, do you start your complaint with "I," such as: "I think" or "I feel?"

	Yes	No
	+1	-1

15. Have you ever thrown things at your partner?

	Yes	No
	-1	+1

16. Do you often engage in name calling or use insults such as "bastard" or "bitch"?

	Yes	No
	-1	+1

17. Do you often say to yourself during an argument with your partner, "I'll get him/her for that?"

	Yes	No
	-1	+1

18. When you complain to your partner, do you usually pinpoint the situation or behavior that bothers you?

	Yes	No
	+1	-1

19. Do you usually ask your partner to

stop doing something that irritates
you instead of suggesting she/he do
something that you would enjoy?

Yes No
-1 +1

20. Do you think you are mostly to blame
for the disharmony in your
relationship?

Yes No
-1 +1

21. Do you believe it's often valuable to
express your anger?

Yes No
+1 -1

22. Can you summarize what your
partner feels or thinks about one of
your pet complaints?

Yes No
+1 -1

23. Do you often yell at your
partner?

Yes No
-1 +1

24. Have you ever hit or slapped your
partner?

Yes No
-1 +1

25. When you're angry, do you usually
call your partner by his/her own
name?

Yes No
+1 -1

26. Do you often say to yourself in an
argument with your partner, "I'll
never let her/him win this one"?

Yes No
-1 +1

27. Do you usually assume you know
what your partner feels and why
he/she says something, without
verifying the accuracy of your
interpretation?

Yes No
-1 +1

28. During a fight with your partner, do
you often say to yourself or out loud,
"It's you or me, baby?"

Yes No
-1 +1

29. When you notice that your fight is
getting out of control, do you know
how to call for a ceasefire?

Yes No
+1 -1

30. Can you tell on which day or at
which moment you or your partner
will likely have a serious fight?

Yes No
+1 -1

Go back over the answers you have given. Total the +1
answers you have circled, then the -1 answers.

Total pluses: + _____ Total minuses: – _____

Now calculate your total fair-fighting score.

If you have more pluses than minuses, your fight patterns are more constructive than destructive. If you have a greater number of minuses than pluses, you should try any one of the plans proposed in this chapter to reduce the destructiveness and increase the constructiveness of your fights.

10

The Effective Division of Work

Len and Ginnie have been married for eight years and have two children, Liz, age seven, and Steve, age four. Len is an insurance man earning $24,000 a year; Ginnie has worked full-time for the past three years, at $13,000 a year, as a secretary in a large hospital. Ginnie convinced Len to join her at a couple-survival course after they started having increasingly bitter fights about the workload each carried.

They still love each other a great deal, enjoy mutually satisfying sexual relations (when they find the time) and share reasonable problem-solving skills; they are also pretty clean fighters. But problems relating to how much each worked inside and outside the home are never resolved satisfactorily. The fights over work are starting to color the positive aspects of their relationship, as is clear in this fight, which took place around six o'clock one Friday night:

LEN (*feeling tired, grumpy and hungry after a long day and a work week of fifty hours*): When do you figure supper will be ready, dear?

GINNIE (*feeling equally tired and grumpy after having worked forty-two hours outside the home and having done what she felt was much more than her share of the housework*): You know, I honestly don't feel hungry right now. Would you mind fixing something for yourself? It would give me time to talk with the kids.

LIZ AND STEVE: Please, Dad. We haven't seen her all week.

LEN (*losing his temper but regretting his outburst immediately*): Listen, folks. I haven't seen much of you either, but I am

169

hungry. I've had one hell of a week and I reckon the least you could do, Ginnie, is fix one meal.

GINNIE *(feeling equally angry and hurt, since she senses Len does not appreciate the work she has put in)*: Listen, sweet, I, too, worked at the office all day. I had to get up last night for Steve who had a nightmare, and this morning at six-thirty to help Liz with her homework. What's more, I didn't get to bed till one in the morning, after having done the laundry and the ironing, prepared the lunchboxes and renewed my driver's licence and our car insurance. You know how to open cans. You know how to turn on the oven, and you know where to find the utensils.

LEN *(feeling somewhat guilty – he had fallen asleep at eight the night before and woken at eight the next morning, so he had not helped Ginnie at all – but still angry and hurt because he thinks Ginnie does not appreciate his contribution)*: You know, the doctor said if I am to control my hypertension I have to sleep more and eat more regularly. Besides, I'm a lousy cook and I'm tired of eating out of cans.

GINNIE *(feeling guilty because she wishes she had more time to cook, but frustrated that, once again, she is being asked to ignore her own fatigue and needs to keep Len and the kids happy)*: Okay, I'll cook now if you'll play with the kids. But I'm fed up with this kind of hassle. I am worried about your health, Len. But what about my doctor's recommendation that I slow down if I am to keep my headaches under control?

LEN *(starting to boil)*: You're fed up! I'm the one who's bringing in most of the salary here.

LIZ: Dad and Mum, stop yelling. *(Steve starts to cry and hugs his mother.)*

GINNIE *(feeling very frustrated and angry)*: Maybe you make more, but you weren't making ends meet until I went back to work. Besides, I work almost as many hours as you do at the office and then put in five times more work than you do at home.

More than 50 per cent of North American households have two full-time breadwinners, so fights of this nature are commonplace. Modern couples face several types of work-related conflicts. We will explore these and some of the solutions couples like Ginnie and Len have found. As you read about the advantages and disadvantages of two-career families, jot down what you consider to be possible solutions to Len and Ginnie's problems.

Dual Career Families: The Advantages

Since the Second World War, women have joined the labor force in ever-increasing numbers. The many advantages of both partners holding jobs outside the home are of six basic types.

Advantage One: Financial. Although women's salaries in North America are about two-thirds those of men, the gap is slowly narrowing. For some couples the wife's revenue is higher than the husband's, because she has more education or training, more marketable skills or has not been affected by layoffs. But these couples are still the exception. The most frequent pattern in North American dual-career families is for the wife's income for full- or part-time work to make up between 30 and 40 per cent of total family revenue. Inflation and slowly diminishing purchasing power have convinced most couples that they could not survive financially without two incomes. Ginnie and Len certainly felt that way.

Advantage Two: Protection against life's catastrophes. Obviously, the dual-career family can better survive unemployment and sickness than can the single-career family. Any income left over after paying family and household expenses can be invested or saved to help in case of the sudden illness or accidental death of a partner, or for retirement. Homemakers in traditional families have been very vulnerable to the premature death of their husband with children to raise, invariably insufficient life insurance and no useful work experience or training to support a family.

The rising divorce rate has made most women but fewer

men aware that a woman's income can be a hedge against the economic catastrophes of divorce. After a separation, women experience far greater economic hardship than men. Despite increasing penalties for nonpayment of support, most former husbands do not pay the support payments awarded by the courts. More than other women, the full-time homemaker, without any financial protection, is "one man away from poverty." Men soon realize that supporting two households is more expensive than supporting one and acknowledge that the salary from the new partner or previous mate can be crucial to financial survival.

Women are starting to think twice before having children, if it means leaving the work force for long. For example, Len wanted to have a third child, but Ginnie reasoned: "If I leave my job for a year or eighteen months, I will lose seniority and salary. That wouldn't be so bad if our marriage lasts, but here we are eight years married and fighting like cats and dogs."

Advantage Three: Self-esteem and mental stimulation. While financial security rates high among the reasons for the female partner to work outside the home, more than half of full-time working women rate out-of-house work as preferable to full-time housework. Moreover, 30 per cent of full-time housewives would prefer to work outside the home for reasons other than financial ones. The responsibility for cooking, child care and homemaking was respected in previous generations, but many women now regard this work as boring and repetitive; it is, therefore, a poor source of self-esteem. Out-of-home work, whether it be manual or white-collar, is seen by most women as more "stimulating" and "worthwhile" than housework. This change in attitude should come as no surprise given increased educational opportunities for women, which have radically changed women's career aspirations. Whereas women were once content with a home and family, they now also aspire to a career. And, as long as they are denied full access to the job market, the greater will be their personal frustration.

Males know that a career can bring self-esteem and mental

stimulation. Apart from the satisfaction of earning money, a career allows a person to meet people besides a partner on a daily basis; gives a person a change of environment; and gains respect from colleagues, bosses and clients for accomplishments.

Advantage Four: Avoidance of the "housewife syndrome." Although our society does not think of a homemaker as "working," the responsibilities of the role are great. Many of the responsibilities, especially those of child-rearing and emotional support of the partner, require exceptional skill and patience. But other, more mundane aspects of the role can produce slowly accumulating frustration and alienation. A house cleaned by ten in the morning will again be in disorder by the time partner and children have been home for an hour – 365 days a year. Not only is the work repetitive, but the homemakers, whether male or female, can easily become frustrated because there is nothing to show for the 365 times they have cleaned the house. So it is with cooking, dishwashing and laundering: at best there is temporary proof of work well done and little room for initiative.

Partners or children who have not done only housework, for even a week, let alone 365 days a year, tend to take it for granted. Moreover, the housewife has to arrange her schedule around everyone else's. If she feels like reading, writing, taking courses or just relaxing, she must slot these activities into her mate's nap time or pursue them when her partner is home, rested, in a good mood and willing to babysit.

"Housewife syndrome" is a term used by psychiatrists to describe homemakers' low-grade depression, mild anxiety about the future, fear of going outside the home, lack of sexual appetite and weight gain or loss. It is not surprising that many women prefer the dual-career option to the housewife role, especially if they have heard their own mothers say: "I should never have married right out of school. I should have had a career; then I would not find myself in the rut I'm in today."

Advantage Five: Equality of roles. When both partners bring in a salary and have responsibilities and sources of stimulation outside the home, chances are increased that both will feel "equal." In many traditional marriages, husband and wife lived in two different worlds – he in the world of "work" and she in the world of "home" – and neither really understood the other's. The partner who brought in the income tended to have more power and control. Usually the male of the household had the major bank account and the female would receive "spending money" from him. He would decide when to change jobs, when to move, when to buy a new house or automobile. Often the female would raise the children and the male would occasionally discipline them. The female in this situation often felt downtrodden and dependent on her mate for money, for intellectual stimulation and for moral support. Yet, interestingly, health statistics show that this traditional division of labor has taken a much greater toll on men's physical health than on women's.

Many couples who have dual careers take pleasure in the fact that their household has no boss. Both partners have their own bank accounts, make decisions together and share child-raising and housework. One drawback of the traditional family was that children saw only their mothers as emotional and dependent; their fathers were perceived to be rational and independent. Girls did not see rational and independent role models, and boys did not see a man able to express emotions, especially dependency and love. In dual-career families, children are more likely to see flexibile roles and are better prepared to meet the unpredictable, multi-faceted demands of life.

Advantage Six: Empathy and respect. When both partners have lived in both worlds of household work and the open job market, there can be an increase in mutual empathy. She will learn how it feels to have a crazy, cold or incompetent boss, to feel the stresses of deadlines and the competitiveness of workmates. He will learn how it feels to do repetitive household chores, to take the children to the doctor and to wake up at night to attend to their needs. With greater empathy can come greater respect and understanding. Moreover, when

174

both partners work outside the home and have a salary and social contacts, there is less risk of one partner taking the other for granted.

Dual-Career Families: The Disadvantages

The dual-career option solves some problems but creates others:

Disadvantage One: Stress-related illnesses. As women have joined the job market, their incidence of stress-related illnesses has gradually caught up with men's. Heart attacks, ulcers, alcoholism and lung cancer used to be predominantly male illnesses, but today women are increasingly prone to these disorders.

Disadvantage Two: Who will do the housework? Housewives work in the home between 35 and 70 hours a week. If you add to these hours all the hours spent in watching over the children – 7 evenings during the week and 2 complete weekend days – the household responsibilities can consume 112 hours per week. If all the housewife's responsibilities – washing, sewing, cleaning, cooking, babysitting and child-rearing – were contracted out, the bill would easily surpass $30,000 a year. When the woman of the house takes a part- or full-time job outside the home, someone has to assume the household duties.

The most frequent topic for fights between dual-career couples is over who will do the housework, although women do more housework than men even when both partners work a similar number of hours outside the home.

Disadvantage Three: Who will be boss? One advantage of traditional family roles is that both partners know who is supposed to be in charge of what. Dual-career families, on the other hand, often simply do not find new ways to approach leadership decisions. As a result, their partnership can sometimes flounder like a boat without a rudder.

Disadvantage Four: What are the roles? Traditional divisions of labor gave each partner a clear idea of the social behavior to adopt with, for example, children and in-laws and with each other. Both partners knew their scripts: the man was expected to be strong, silent, rational, independent and a disciplinarian. The woman was expected to be less dominant, more talkative, emotional, dependent and loving. Partners in dual-career relationships find that they often have to write a new script. If they don't, both may assume or refuse to assume one role. For example, both may become strong and silent and good child disciplinarians, but neither may supply love and affection to the children.

Disadvantage Five: Work overload. One of the most common complaints of dual-career partners is overwork. If both partners work, say, forty hours a week and commute for six, someone will be taking care of the children while the parents are at work, but there will still be fifty to seventy hours of work to be done at home. One consequence of a heavy workload is that the finer things of life – chatting, playing with the children, listening to music, making love or having a healthy fight – become rare. The suggestion that two-career couples spend time in discussion, problem-solving, listening to each other or sensual caresses invariably elicits the response: "Great idea, but when? There's no time." In dual-career families money may not be a rare resource, but time, and especially quality time spent together, is. To be sure, during vacations neither partner may work for one, two or even three weeks. But in their "real world," it is mostly work and very little play.

Possible Solutions for the Dual-Career Couple

Ginnie summed up the dilemma of dual-career families this way: "I feel I'm damned if I keep my job, and damned if I stay at home." She and Len conducted a problem-solving exercise on the issues that had been causing their work-related fights.

Problems according to Ginnie:
1. Len does not do his share of work around the house.
2. Len takes my secretarial work for granted and does not appreciate the salary I bring in.
3. We do not share enough fun time together.
4. We do not spend enough time with the children.
5. We waste too much money.

Problems according to Len:
1. Since Ginnie went back to work, she has changed. She is less loving and less fun to be with and she doesn't appreciate my work.
2. Ginnie does not want to have another child. I do.
3. Ginnie thinks I don't do enough housework, and I feel that I do plenty.
4. The children need more time with us than we've been giving them.

Before they could generate possible solutions, they needed to know exactly how they spent their work time and their combined income. Len and Ginnie filled out two sets of self-monitoring forms: the Couple Workload Self-Monitoring form and the Couple Financial Self-Monitoring form.

It takes about five minutes a day to fill out the Couple Workload Self-Monitoring form. When it is complete, it will provide you with an accurate record of how much time you spend on various kinds of work at home and outside the home. Mark the time spent every day on each activity. Once you have completed your schedule for one week, fill in the "Usual total" column, estimating how much time you usually spend on each activity. Finally, estimate how much time you think your partner normally spends on each item listed.

Couple Workload Self-Monitoring Form

	Time in hours M T W T F S S	Total per week	Usual total	Estimate of partner's time
1. Working outside the home				
2. Commuting				
3. Cooking				
4. Cleaning the house				
5. Doing the laundry				
6. Washing dishes				
7. Buying food and house supplies				
8. Working on the budget				
9. Paying bills				
10. Caring for the children's physical needs				
11. Helping the children with their homework				

(continued on next page)

(continued)

12. Babysitting										
13. Changing beds										
14. Repairing house or appliances										
15. Making home improvements										
16. Repairing the car										
17. Caring for pets										
18. Preparing income-tax returns and other financial/legal matters										
19. Looking after parents and in-laws										
20. Taking courses to improve career prospects										
21. Organizing vacations										
22. Shopping for gifts										
23. Shopping for luxury items										
24. Other										

Weekly Workload Summary Form

	You	Your Partner
Total time spent on work outside the home		
Total time spent on commuting		
Total time spent on educational pursuits		
Total time spent on housework		
TOTAL		

Couple Financing Self-Monitoring Form

Date:_____

Net revenue per month: He $_____

She $_____

Other income: $_____

TOTAL MONTHLY REVENUE: $_____

Monthly Expenditures

Mortgage or rent payments	$
Food shopping	$
Food at restaurants	$
Cigarettes	$
Liquor	$
Clothing	$
Insurance (life, house and car)	$
Electricity	$
Gas	$
House repairs	$
Car repairs	$

(continued on next page)

(continued)

Furniture repairs	$
Heat	$
Transportation	$
Dentist	$
Doctor	$
Medication	$
Appliances	$
Club fees	$
Education and books	$
Retirement savings plans	$
Loan payments	$
Babysitters' fees	$
Gifts	$
Luxury items	$
Other (e.g. Entertainment, etc.)	$
TOTAL	$

Like most couples, Len and Ginnie got some interesting surprises from filling in these forms. Their workload estimates were pretty much in agreement, but Len was impressed by how many hours a week Ginnie spent doing housework. Len spent three weeknights and one half day on sports activities. He also watched fifteen hours of television a week. For one of the evenings when Len was absent, they agreed to hire a babysitter so that Ginnie could go to the movies with friends. However, during twenty-one of the hours Len practised a sport or watched television, Ginnie was doing housework or helping the children with their homework. Len noted, too, that most evenings (for a total of seven hours a week) he took a nap and read his newspaper; Ginnie worked for five of these hours. In total, Len worked and traveled fifty-six hours a week outside the home and worked an average of ten hours inside the house, for a total of sixty-six hours. Ginnie worked forty-six hours out-side the home and thirty-two inside for a total of seventy-eight hours.

The financial self-monitoring form also led to some interest-ing surprises. With Ginnie's $10,000 annual income after taxes, and Len's $18,000, they had $28,000 available a year, or $2,333 a month. Their expenses were $1,800 a month. With the excess they had paid off two personal loans; for the past six months they had an average of $533 available to put into savings to buy nonessentials or to make home improvements. Ginnie, who usually left the budgeting to Len, was pleasantly surprised by how large the monthly surplus was. Len knew it was a pretty reasonable amount, but he was also surprised.

With these statistics in hand, the couple could undertake more realistic problem solving. Len and Ginnie worked their way through the problems on their original problem-definition lists and came up with some proposed solutions.

Problem definition: Len has expected more cooking from Ginnie, but Ginnie works an average of twelve hours a week more than Len	
Possible solutions	*Whose idea*
1. Len learns how to cook	Len's
2. We hire someone to help with the housework so Ginnie can cook more often	Ginnie's
3. Len drops one outing a week and helps more with the housework	Len's
4. Ginnie cuts her full-time job to half-time	Len's
5. Len works fewer hours on his job and spends more time working at home	Ginnie's
6. We both work less outside the home	Ginnie's
7. We spend less on luxury goods	Len's

Len and Ginnie decided on a step-by-step approach: for six months they would adopt solutions 1, 2 and 7. Len would cook two nights a week; and they would employ a housecleaner for one half day, so Ginnie could be free to cook two more nights a week. They would also forgo buying a second television, new furniture and downhill-ski equipment. Both felt comfortable with these solutions but agreed to monitor their plan weekly.

Both partners felt that their work inside and outside the home was unappreciated by their mate. Each felt the other should show more appreciation and understanding but, engulfed by feelings of resentment, each had stifled interest in the other's work.

By using their active-listening and self-disclosure skills (Chapter Three), they increased their understanding for each other's work. By helping each other problem solve (Chapter Six) on job-related difficulties, they could increase respect and support for each other; and by flexing their verbal appreciation skills, they could help their partner feel less taken for granted (Chapter Four).

Len later commented: "I realize now that if I don't express appreciation for all Ginnie does around here, she may keep on doing it, but she'll greatly resent me. And I wouldn't blame her."

Ginnie responded: "Now that Len has talked more about his job, and I have actually listened to him, I realize that he not only works longer hours than I do outside the home, but his hours are often much more demanding than mine. He has to exert himself constantly to sell. I have stress periods at work, too, but far less frequently."

A third problem each recognized was that they had little time for each other. "We are becoming more and more like business partners," said Len, "and we have less time for fun." Both decided that, within the year, they would cut on expenses enough to allow them to work fewer hours. After all, they said: "You only live once." In the interim, they agreed to reserve at least one evening a week to be together.

The final problem Len and Ginnie faced concerned their children. Both felt they were not giving Steve and Liz enough time, love or discipline. Ginnie wished Len would become more involved:

GINNIE: We both discipline the children when they're naughty, but I wish you would help more often with Liz's homework and spend more time just playing and talking with both of them.

LEN: Well, I really feel incapable when helping Liz with her homework. You're so much better than I am at it. And you know me, I have trouble talking to the kids. I never know what to say. They have their world and I have mine. I feel the same about play. Steve and I just don't enjoy doing the same things.

Being a parent is not easy. We are not born with parenting skills anymore than we are born with the ability to forge a happy marriage. Len had to learn to stop saying, "I don't know how to be a more loving father." Instead he had to say, "I want to learn." Ginnie had to admit that because of her family background, she had entered marriage with a greater ability to play, talk and work with children than had Len. As a result, the children tended to be more affectionate to and appreciative of her. Once she recognized this, Ginnie learned to be patient with Len's efforts to become more involved with the children, and she verbally encouraged him more often for his efforts to change.

Different Problems Demand Different Solutions

Each couple must find solutions to their work-related problems that best fit their situation. Ginnie and Len decided to follow the dual-career option; other couples will seek different solutions. Some, for example, will be happier if only one person works outside the home and the other assumes most of the housework. Whether the woman or the man becomes the homemaker, problems are bound to arise. Some women and men prefer to spend most of their work hours in the home, especially when the children are young; and there are many advantages to this option if the couple can afford it. Sometimes these couples will keep expenses low to permit themselves the

184

luxury of only one partner working outside the home. Other couples have opted for a dual-career relationship for, among other things, its greater purchasing power. As Len and Ginnie found out, however, energy invested in making money to enjoy a "better standard of living" can conflict with the quality of the relationships among partners and their children. If two partners don't maintain the quality of their relationship, the money they worked so hard to earn may be spent on divorce lawyers.

Couples must keep work in perspective and not let it dominate their relationship; but partners must also appreciate each other's work and not take their efforts for granted. Partners exercising their listening skills can get an honest taste of how the other's workday feels. Even better would be to change roles, even if only temporarily. If, for example, one partner has looked after certain household responsibilities, let the other partner take on the tasks for a given period of time. (In Ginnie and Len's case, Len did the cooking and shopping and helped the children with their homework for a week, and Ginnie managed the budget, paid the bills, cut the grass and took out the garbage.) If possible, it helps to meet the people your partner works with and to spend a day or two with him/her in the workplace.

Three New Work Options
In some couples, both partners have half-time jobs outside the home. This arrangement can help them to avoid being exhausted, and also permits more free time for work and play at home. Of course, not all couples can survive for lengthy periods on part-time salaries. For them, the "your-turn-my-turn" option may be an answer. One partner works full-time outside the home, while the other works at home. Then, after a few months or years, the partners switch. This arrangement requires great role flexibility, but it can be extremely rewarding.

With the dissolution of the extended family, couples now rely increasingly on each other for needs that used to be met by siblings, parents or children. Couples who know how to take advantage of outside support systems – public-service agencies, friends, self-help groups and religious organizations – have a much better chance of surviving the stresses of life: illness, unemployment, death or financial hardship. Some couples and their children, if they have them, form support systems made up of other couples and singles. These groups exchange babysitting, equipment and car pools. They can also involve sharing living accommodation and pooling financial resources. Although many independent-minded couples turn up their noses at such exchanges of social and emotional support, their disdain can lead to a discord or even to a rupture of their relationship.

11

Open Marriage or Monogamy: The Pros and Cons

Wayne is a thirty-four-year-old high-school teacher and his wife, Fey, is a thirty-one-year-old nurse; one evening, Wayne had an outbreak of jealous rage, and their marriage was in trouble:

FEY: I'm not sure what is going to happen to us. Three years ago, at Wayne's insistence, we opened up our marriage. He had been reading O'Neill's book[8] on open marriage and suggested that we try it. I felt very hurt that he would want to have sex with another woman. I was sure that he was bored with me and wanted to start playing the field. At first I did nothing. I had been raised to think that if you were married, you put all your eggs in one basket, and I felt very much in love with Wayne and our two children.

WAYNE: Fey's right. I started the ball rolling. I had been taking a sociology course, and I wrote a paper on alternatives to traditional marriage. When I broached the subject with Fey, I honestly felt it would do our relationship some good. We had been married for five years and had dated for five years before that. Although we have always had a good time, Fey was gradually showing less interest than I was in the sexual aspect of the relationship. I figured those books plugging open marriage must be right, that all your needs cannot be satisfied by one person. I thought our chances of lasting as a couple would increase if we tried to be less dependent on each other.

FEY: Wayne was so enthusiastic about trying it out that I didn't want to deny him his freedom. I figured I would lose more by being a chicken about it than if I braved it out.

WAYNE: I promised Fey that she and the kids would always come first for me, that if I did have relations with another woman, I would not let it infringe on our relationship. Well, as Fey knows, I have had relations with two other women. She knows who, when and how often. As I promised, these affairs have been casual and I don't think they interfered with our relationship.

FEY: He's right. I came to realize that I had been making a mountain out of a molehill. He was very decent about his affairs and I never felt he was trying to hurt me or make me jealous. But, after two years of this marriage that was only open on his side, I found myself becoming attracted to one of the residents at the hospital where I work. I didn't tell Wayne about Ken because I didn't know quite how to do it. I started seeing Ken one night a month. At first I was curious and just out to have fun, like Wayne had said. But after about four months, I found myself thinking about Ken more and more often, and I wanted to see him more frequently.

WAYNE: I finally woke up to what was happening when Fey and I and Ken were all at the Christmas party at the hospital. Fey and Ken danced together often and very closely – no necking, mind you. A physical therapist on the hospital staff, someone with whom I grew up, took it upon himself to inform me that my wife had been having a torrid affair with this guy for more than a year. I hadn't even suspected. At around midnight I suggested that Fey and I go home. She agreed, unwillingly, and the fight started in the car.

FEY: To me, it was a typical double standard. Mister Liberated, here, was hot on an open marriage as long as it was one-sided; as soon as I got into the action he became jealous.

WAYNE (his voice rising): When I had my flings I did not become romantically involved. You should have seen Fey and this guy together. She told me all about him – how he and I are different, how she likes me for certain reasons and him for others. I'm not sure I can stand it.

FEY: The whole experience has been a real eye-opener for me. It has been two weeks since the situation exploded. I haven't seen Ken since, except for a few moments. I don't know what I'm going to do. I feel very confused: I don't want to give up my relationship with Ken, but I can't stand the tension at home. Wayne has never been like this before. He is brooding and touchy; he yells a lot. The kids are only two and five, but they know something is wrong. I just don't know what I am going to do. I can't help but feel that this would never have happened if Wayne had not started it all.

WAYNE: But I said I wouldn't fall in love with someone else and I didn't.

FEY: I can't control my feelings like that. Besides, I don't understand how you can go to bed with someone just for sex. I have to feel closeness and respect for someone before I am turned on.

During the past twenty years, there has been a significant increase in sexual experimentation by married couples in North America. There are various forms of open marriage: for some couples one or another form works; for others monogamy is the best alternative. But there are questions that partners can ask themselves in attempting to decide on an arrangement that suits them best.

As Fey and Wayne came to realize, the issue is not whether a couple has a monogamous or open relationship, but how well each partner's needs for sexual fulfillment, personal growth, self-expression and emotional security are satisfied, and how conducive the relationship is to shared trust, child-rearing and open communication. Monogamous and open marriages fulfill certain needs, but each also generates problems that must be solved if the relationship is to survive.

In this chapter we will meet several couples and come to know their experiences with open marriage and monogamy, and the arrangements they ultimately negotiated.

From the occasional fling to partner-swapping arrangements, sexual relations outside the original couple are becoming more common. Such changes in sexual values are linked to societal changes. The extended family was typical of western society until the 1940s: the family was headed by mother and father, whose roles as housewife and breadwinner were clearly defined, and subsequent generations usually lived close by if not actually under the same roof. With technological changes, couples began to go from their "homes" to where the work was. Increased mobility reduced the stability and importance of the extended family: husband and wife were on their own, cut off from their parents and siblings.

During the past thirty years, increased affluence and more leisure time have allowed couples to concentrate on more than financial survival. Our society has gone through a sexual revolution, and the media have capitalized on this change in values by bombarding the public with sex and romance to sell products, images and literature, art, films, music, fashion and theater.

Changes for women – better education, improved job status, financial independence and effective birth control – have altered the traditional husband-wife relationship. Unlike marriages of the past, in which the male was dominant and the female was submissive, today couples tend to be two individuals with roughly equivalent resources, who decide to form a union for as long as it is satisfying to them. These partners, like more traditional couples, concentrate on maintaining emotional and financial security and on child-rearing; however, they also demand scope for personal growth and self-expression. Previous generations assumed that when they took marriage vows, they abandoned certain alternatives; however, many couples of the sixties, seventies and eighties sincerely hope that they will not have to sacrifice individual needs and goals for their marriage.

Open Marriage

Extramarital relationships have been described as "group marriage," "open marriage," "infidelity," "adultery," "multilateral relations," "co-marital sex" and "spouse-swapping." The experience of sexual relationships outside a marriage can vary greatly, and partners must evaluate the different forms of extramarital relationships and examine their suitability to the particular needs as individuals and as a couple.

Do not be surprised if you find that you would rather read this chapter by yourself, and if you do not feel like discussing all aspects of your answers with your partner. The question of open marriage touches some very private issues: personal identity and identy as a partner; personal expectations and expectations as part of a couple; personal growth and growth as a pair.

To best identify your feelings about open relationships, read each question below and formulate your own response. Then read the discussions that follow each question.

1. What need(s) do you hope to answer by having an extramarital relationship?
2. How important will the new relationship be?
3. Does an extramarital relationship hurt or enhance your original relationship?
4. Are feelings, values and reactions concerning extramarital activities discussed openly between the partners?
5. How visible are the extramarital activities to family and friends?
6. Who is "fair game"?
7. Do both partners participate?
8. Should the rules governing extramarital activities be negotiated? If so, what rules should be used?

One: What need(s) do you hope to answer by having an extramarital relationship? Most people assume that the principal motive for extramarital relationships is sex; in fact, however, the reasons are more complex. Partners fantasize about open marriage, try it out and keep their relationship open to satisfy needs that they feel were not fully satisfied by a monogamous relationship.

A desire for more variety, frequency and quality of sexual contact is very often cited as the motivation for opening a relationship. (As we have seen in Chapter Five, the intensity of the human pleasure response is partly dependent upon variation.) Partners who have been married for several years often find that the intensity and frequency of their sexual responsiveness have declined. Some react to this decline with great alarm; others easily accept that making love to the same person year in and year out cannot be as exciting as it was on the first encounter. Others react like Wayne: "Sex with Fey was great – when it happened. She tended to be less interested than I and, instead of pressuring her constantly, I proposed that I have the occasional fling providing that my extramarital activities would not detract from our sex life."

In general, men tend to separate sexual pleasure from their desire to satisfy other needs. Women tend not to distinguish sexual from emotional responses. When Fey decided to become involved with Ken, it was partly for sexual variation but more out of curiosity: "I wondered what it would be like to make love with another man who attracted me physically. I also found Ken warm and understanding, and he treated me with more respect than Wayne ever had. He seemed to value my opinion more."

For many women and some men, wanting to open up a marriage can be a need to satisfy a curiosity about new experiences and needs such as respect, enhancement of self-esteem, understanding and warmth.

The different behavior of men and women is not determined biologically. In the past ten years, as women have become more assertive and gained more job opportunities and financial security, increasing numbers of women are initiating open marriage mainly for sexual variation.

Some partners, like Fey, want extramarital relationships to gain acceptance and approval from someone other than their mate. Most of us need some feedback from the outside world to feel worthwhile. Monogamous partners often have an implicit understanding that most of their positive feedback will come from their partner. However, signs of such respect may be too habitual or too seldom to be reinforcing. Fey felt that Wayne appreciated her for her sex appeal and for their beautiful children but that he had little respect for her emotional strength or her intellect.

Those who lack self-confidence may crave frequent confirmations that someone other than their partner finds them attractive. Such a person will often place enormous importance on his/her physical appearance and may be quite flirtatious. Once seduction is complete, it is time to move on, for when the sex object has said, "Yes, I'll make love to you," he/she is lowered in the seducer's eyes: "Anyone who accepted me can't be all that great."

Although some have a lifelong search for self-confidence, others go through brief periods of self-doubt. These may or may not be related to what is happening in their original relationship. For example, a woman, after bearing several children, may feel compelled to prove – with a man other than her husband – that she is still attractive as a woman. People who have experienced illness or failure or who feel overcome by the awareness that they are aging may seek confirmation of their worth and attractiveness from someone other than their partner.

In some relationships, unresolved hostility generates the need to experiment. A husband or wife takes a lover to punish the spouse for some wrongdoing. The partner is not spared any of the gory details about the lovers. Especially important are descriptions of the ways in which the new lover is superior to the spouse: "He's so virile, but gentle and understanding." "She's so responsive – in and out of bed." Punishing the spouse is more important than the new lover.

Those who crave stimulation and unpredictability may engage in extramarital affairs just to keep from becoming bored or depressed. The sexual challenge, the new activities, new subjects of conversation and the new friends that come with the new partner can all be important sources of varied stimulation.

Finally, some embark on extramarital activities hoping that the new relationship will satisfy many of their emotional needs. A marriage in which one or both partners no longer find their partner attractive sexually, intellectually or emotionally may prompt such an "affair." There may be a tacit or overt agreement that the union will not be dissolved legally, but the partners no longer expect their relationship to be their principal source of sexual and emotional pleasure.

Two: How important will the new relationship be? How much time is spent with the new partner? Does the new relationship compete with the old for available time? How much energy does the new relationship require, not only the energy spent with the lover but also the energy spent thinking about him/her, making plans or covering tracks? How much time and energy do the original partners devote to discussion of extramarital relationships and their impact on the original relationship?

It is virtually impossible not to compare the investment of time and energy in the extramarital affair with that invested in the original relationship. For example, Wayne devoted relatively little time and energy to extramarital relationships compared with his relationship with Fey. Although Fey started her extramarital activities later, her new relationship was consuming more time and energy than Wayne's.

Three: Does an extramarital relationship hurt or enhance your original relationship? Many who extol the virtues of open marriage hold that extramarital affairs actually enhance the original relationship. They suggest that it is impossible for one relationship to answer all emotional and sexual needs. Traditional marriage, they argue, often leads to frustration and divorce (legal, emotional or both), because the participants expect too many of their important needs to be satisfied by one partner.

It is not humanly possible, they argue, for one person to satisfy another's emotional, social, sexual and intellectual needs for an extended period of time. Once a couple has developed a solid emotional base and strong channels of communication, their primary emotional growth will continue within the confines of the original relationship; but significant needs, whether sexual, emotional, intellectual or social, will be satisfied outside the relationship. This school of thought holds that most mature individuals experience an improvement in the quality and stability of the original relationship when these needs are satisfied elsewhere. Open marriage can be a solution to problems such as sexual habituation, boredom with routine, lack of growth and lack of challenge or novelty.

There are also many ways in which open marriage may detract from the original relationship: jealousy, depression, insecurity, resentful competition between original partners, severe constraints on time spent with the original partner and family, financial strains on the family, lack of sexual interest in the spouse, increased hostility and increased stress level for both spouses.

Four: Are feelings, values and reactions concerning extramarital activities discussed openly between the partners? A classic double standard often occurred in traditional marriages: the wife stayed home, kept house and was monogamous; the husband, who was much more geographically and socially mobile, participated in extramarital liaisons. This pattern was rarely discussed openly between partners; sometimes there was a tacit understanding that what she didn't know wouldn't hurt her. Couples who engage in partner swapping are the other extreme.

Between these types fall couples like Wayne and Fey, who tell each other about some but not all aspects of their extramarital relationships. Some couples find extramarital affairs more satisfying if each reports back the details to the spouse; others may agree not to be informed about what happened, when or with whom.

Five: How visible are the extramarital activities to family and friends? Some couples are willing to embark on an open marriage provided that children, neighbors, in-laws, parents and colleagues are not aware of their activities. (Part of Wayne's anger at Fey was triggered by the "humiliation that everyone knew but me.") Some couples are particularly concerned that their children's image of them as a loving and loyal couple not be shaken.

Six: Who is "fair game"? Some can accept and even be enthusiastic about their partner's extramarital activities provided the new lover is not a next-door neighbor, an in-law, a sibling, a babysitter and so on. Each couple must set the guidelines – and stick to them.

Seven: Do both partners participate? Proponents of open marriage emphasize that both partners should want and participate in extramarital activities for the arrangement to be successful. When the "openness" is one-sided, the partner who does not participate may feel dependent, trapped, insecure, unloved and sexually unsatisfied. The experimenting partner might take the spouse for granted or lose respect for him/her.

Any imbalance increases the risk of hostility. For example, Wayne and Fey were surprised to find that, although they had agreed to open marriage on what they thought were equal terms, Fey reacted to the new experience very differently than did Wayne. Couples who stand by equal standards in principle but use a double standard in practice run such risks. In their discussions on open marriage, Wayne had answered Fey's fears that she would be jealous of his other partners by saying, "That's a completely irrational reaction – you'll get over it." Jealousy did become an important factor, but much to their surprise, it was Wayne's problem, not Fey's.

Eight: Should the rules governing the extramarital activities be negotiated? If so, what rules should be used? In Chapter Seven, we discussed negotiating skills and compromise. Couples tend to negotiate either formally or informally: some purposefully negotiate their way through delicate situations; others compromise without consciously acknowledging it. Couples who negotiate an open marriage can often avoid some of the negative consequences of extramarital activities if they agree on well-defined guidelines for behavior. Their "contract" can cover what they believe will be all the potential gains and risks of extramarital relationships. These eight questions may serve as a suitable basis for negotiation.

Jim and Betty, whom we met in Chapter Three, found that relationships outside their marriage were placing severe stress on their relationship. Therefore, they negotiated the following agreement to cover their extramarital activities.

1. We agree that each can have relationships with other partners for fun, not to replace the original partner as number one.
2. Neither of us will allow any extramarital activity to take time and energy away from our marriage.
3. If one or both of us feels that extramarital relationships are detracting from our relationship, we will discuss this subject and be open to changes in this contract.
4. From time to time, we will generally inform each other about our activities. However, we agree that we will not discuss details of our affairs.
5. We will both make every attempt to keep our affairs entirely private so that they are not brought to the attention of family, friends or colleagues.
6. Both of us plan to be open to extramarital sexual relationships.
7. Either of us is free to request a re-evaluation of this contract at any time. The quality of our marriage depends on us both accepting each of the rules we have set down, but we will both stay open to negotiation should a change in our situations require it.

Neither Betty nor Jim signed their contract, and it was not legally binding; but there are advantages to this type of informal arrangement, whether written or verbal. Such a contract requires frank discussion of the dimensions of open marriage and allows each spouse to express preferences as to how various situations should be handled.

Wayne and Fey urgently needed to review their arrangement because Wayne felt Fey had violated their original agreement; Fey felt ambivalent about her marital relationship, her extramarital relationship and their original decision. Jim and Betty were able to reduce the emotional distance between them by holding frank discussions and hammering out their contract.

If you and your partner are considering extramarital experimentation, each of you might answer the eight basic questions and compare your answers. Negotiate compromises if you can and, if you wish, write an agreement. Examining your plans closely will ensure that both of you begin your new lifestyle with your eyes open.

Jealousy: When Is It Dangerous and When Is It Healthy?

Although some marriages can be enriched through an open arrangement, some are unaltered; others are destroyed. Success or deterioration of a relationship depends on many complex factors and is difficult to predict. Partners' personalities, the ways they interact, and their life circumstances will strongly influence the outcome.

One of the main stumbling blocks of extramarital relations is jealousy. Most people have been jealous at one time or another, but it is not an emotion that is easily defined: painful, uncomfortable, distracting, disorienting. "He loves her more than me." "She is giving what I deserve to someone else." "How dare he humiliate me?" "How dare she share herself with someone else?" Jealous thoughts often include pessimistic predictions: "I'll lose him." "She will stop loving me." "I will be second best." "People will say I'm a fool."

Jealousy may bruise one's self-image: "It's because I'm not beautiful." "I'm not lovable." "I'm not a good enough lover." "I'm not intelligent enough, mysterious enough, powerful enough." A jealous partner may lash out at the "unfaithful" mate: "cheater," "tramp," "hypocrite," "traitor" or even "lucky to be able to find other lovers."

The reaction of jealous lovers depends on their personalities, their partners' personalities, how strong the feelings of jealousy are and their perception of the situation. Some, like Betty, boil inside; others, like Fey, agree to tolerate their mate's affairs with reservations. Some, like Wayne, fly into rages, hurling insults, threats, tears and promises. Jealousy may motivate some to take a lover to "even the score" and to prove their own worth. In extreme cases, victims of jealousy may attempt suicide, motivated by a strong desire to punish or to be saved by their partner.

Some people love their partner dearly, yet seldom, if ever, feel jealous. Others are jealous and possessive not only of their partner's real or imagined lovers, but also of their job, health, appearance, hobbies, relationship with the children and so on. Most of us fall somewhere between the nonchalant partner and the compulsively jealous partner. What of the Bettys and Waynes of this world, who never felt jealous until their partner engaged in extramarital relationships? They have five basic options:

1. to negotiate or renegotiate the rules governing extramarital activities;
2. to ask the experimenting partner to return to monogamy;
3. to concentrate on achieving better control over jealous feelings and behavior;
4. to find ways of improving the relationship to diminish the threat of extramarital activities;
5. to terminate the present relationship and look for a new, more compatible partner.

Wayne's jealousy provoked a serious examination of the strengths and weaknesses of his marriage to Fey. Each of them aired their grievances and pinpointed the things that they liked about themselves, each other and their relationship. As their relationship improved through the survival skills they learned, Fey began to be less interested in her lover and felt that Wayne was satisfying more of her needs. They renegotiated their open-marriage arrangement and agreed to limit their contact with others to a maximum of once per month. As well, both promised that if either felt their marriage was severely threatened by extramarital activities, they would discuss the situation immediately.

In the two years since Fey and Wayne weathered their crisis, they are still together and still "open," without apparent damaging consequences:

WAYNE: I realized that in part my jealousy was due to my immaturity, and I did have a double standard. But once I aired my feelings with Fey, I understood that I didn't want to deprive her of her freedom. I want her to stay with me; but because she wants to stay with me, not because I forbid her to leave or because she feels I need to be protected. I think that since our crisis, I have worked a lot harder on myself and our relationship in order to be a more interesting and interested partner. I am convinced that our experiments in open marriage have helped us.

Fey also found the open marriage positive, but she emphasized that her relationship with her lover had taught her that men other than Wayne could satisfy her needs. Although she finds her relationship with Wayne very satisfying, she does not assume that it will always be.

Intense Unresolved Jealousy

Milton, a forty-three-year-old lawyer, and Phyllis, a twenty-eight-year-old business-school graduate, lived an upper-middle-class life in a city. They had been married for three years and had a one-year-old child. Milton's twelve-year-old son from a previous marriage also lived with them. Phyllis had resigned from a promising position in a large marketing company to raise their child and look after the home.

The couple had met at work and had enjoyed a "rich and exciting romance" for six months. Milton said that he had found Phyllis so "interesting, exciting, sexy and beautiful that I left my wife to marry her." Phyllis said that she, too, had given up a five-year-long relationship; she fell in love with Milton for his "charm, jetset lifestyle, maturity and sense of direction."

Their marriage seemed to be running quite smoothly until Milton informed Phyllis that he was having a casual affair with a woman in another city, but it "meant nothing." Phyllis was very jealous and angry at Milton's confession, and they fought openly about the affair.

MILTON: I refuse to clip my wings for any woman. I give you

love, a great income, children, the chance to travel and a great future. How can you refuse me a little fling?

PHYLLIS: I can't help but feel that if you keep this up, sooner or later we'll be through.

When Phyllis found that her migraines and insomnia were made much worse by Milton's revelation and their fight, she decided to consult a psychotherapist.

For a year, Phyllis's psychotherapist helped her to understand the roots of her low self-confidence, tension and jealousy. She began to develop more self-confidence and independence after carefully analyzing the ways in which she relied on Milton. She started to work part-time to reduce her financial dependence, joined an aerobic dance group and started to meet men socially.

After about nine months of therapy, her psychotherapist and Milton agreed that her jealousy over Milton could be alleviated if "she had the occasional lover." Phyllis agreed to try it. However, her jealousy did not subside after two "pretty entertaining affairs." Their conflict was about two incompatible preferences and ended in a stalemate.

There are three ways to break such a stalemate:

1. Evaluate the pros and cons of open and closed marriage. Then, after careful discussion and examination of the alternatives, see if you still both hold the same points of view.
2. Work to enhance life together in the areas where there is room for improvement: sensuality, expression of affection, leisure time and division of work.
3. If the first two options are unacceptable to one or both of you, consider a constructive separation.

Milton and Phyllis had considered these options:

MILTON: I really feel Phyllis is being silly and immature. She doesn't need to feel jealous just because I am having an affair with another woman.

PHYLLIS: Milton, I can't forget that our own relationship started as a "casual affair," which eventually blossomed into your separation and our marriage. I think we should open up about why we both have come to our decisions. The second option could also interest me. But I refuse to go to any sessions unless Milton agrees to suspend his affair.

MILTON: Okay, I'll accept your ultimatum. I won't see my girlfriend for two months, but I have never believed in this couple-therapy stuff. Improving our love life or how we divide up the work simply does not interest me and it wouldn't change a thing. However, an evaluation of the pros and cons of open marriage would be a good thing. I have a hunch Phyllis might become more rational about it if she took the time to understand why I want our marriage to be open.

PHYLLIS: I'll agree to consider your reasons carefully; but, frankly, I will be surprised if I change my mind.

Milton and Phyllis completed a detailed analysis of the rational and emotional implications of open marriage.

Phyllis's Analysis	
Pros	Cons
Milton will be happier in the long run. I could have fun with other men. We would have peace at home, at least temporarily. Our marriage may last longer.	I feel jealous and angry. I think Milton should put the energy into our relationship. I think Milton and I should be willing to improve our own relationship, so he won't need another woman. If Milton continues to look for romantic involvement outside our marriage, he will eventually want to marry another woman. I would rather change partners while I'm still young and have only one child.

Milton's Analysis	
Pros	Cons
Phyllis should see that this will help, not hurt our relationship.	Phyllis is jealous.
	Phyllis is angry.
It would do Phyllis good to have the occasional fling. I can't satisfy all her needs.	Phyllis might end our relationship.
I know that I will be miserable if I don't feel free to roam at times.	
I'll be a better father and husband if I don't feel trapped.	
You only live once and everyone should be able to enjoy their life to the hilt.	

After a similar review of monogamy, Milton and Phyllis had the following discussion:

PHYLLIS: Honestly, I think I would be a fool to go along with this open-marriage bit. If Milton is determined to have his cake and eat it too, I would rather we parted. He can do it on his own time.

MILTON: I'm really disappointed. I thought I married a gutsy lady. I really don't think you love me all that much if you won't let me have my little flings.

PHYLLIS: If I really thought they were "little flings" I wouldn't be so concerned, but I think the writing is on the wall.

Their final decision was to separate.

What needs does an open marriage satisfy that might also be satisfied through modifications of a monogamous relationship? Clearly, the needs that a partner or couple hope to satisfy through extramarital activities are those needs that are not satisfied in the monogamous relationship. Milton wanted sexual variety and freedom in an open marriage; he was firmly convinced that no alteration in his relationship with Phyllis would meet these needs. Fey realized her lover was fulfilling needs that could be met in her marriage if her relationship with Wayne changed.

Extramarital contacts are a way out of total dependence on one's mate for all intimate contact. However, it is only one of many types of outside satisfaction. A fulfilling career, an independent hobby, friends of either sex and independent intellectual pursuits are all alternative sources of stimulation. Fulfilling certain needs independent of a partner reduces one's vulnerability to the ups and downs of the relationship. Financial problems, work demands, illness, arguments and so on are less devastating if each partner has other resources to fall back on.

Independent activities can also help partners to appreciate each other, and to reduce the damaging effects of habituation. Independent activities, social contacts, interests – even a planned separation of a few days or weeks – will help partners keep the variety in their relationship.

Some partners will need lots of variation to stay happy; others are satisfied with less. Some people will experience a strong need for emotional and sexual novelty; others are satisfied with what one person can offer. The closer are their needs for variety, the more likely partners will be able to agree on a lifestyle.

Conflict between partners over open or closed marriage is often really a conflict over needs for security and stimulation. Someone who values security much more than stimulation will frequently conflict with a partner who values stimulation much more than security. Monogamy, open marriage or separation – none provides a magic resolution of these basic differences. A couple must decide which choice is best for them and work hard to make the most of their choice.

12

Separation or Divorce: Coping with the Crisis

Parents and children can be happier and better adjusted after a constructive divorce than during an unstable marriage. Yet many couples do not attempt a temporary or permanent separation because they fear the effects on themselves and their children. Partners can approach the question of whether to separate constructively. This chapter deals with considerations that affect the decision; options open to partners who are considering separation but have not committed themselves to it; and solutions for the problems that recently separated partners often experience.

Fred, forty-five, was a pudgy, neatly dressed dentist from a working-class background. His wife Donna, thirty-four, was a very attractive, well-dressed woman from a middle-class background. They had two sons and one daughter ranging in age from four to eleven. Fred had been married while a dental student, but his first wife had left him for another man two years after he graduated. He and Donna, his dental technician, had lived together for several years and married when Donna became pregnant with their first child.

FRED: My wife's furious. She's called a lawyer and threatened to kick me out of the house and freeze my bank accounts. She has told my parents and our friends that I'm an adulterer. I am totally confused and upset. All I've worked so hard to build is falling apart. I never thought Donna would act this way. My practice has been losing money and I recently made some bad investments. I just borrowed $50,000 to pay my debts and office expenses.

DONNA (*looking cool, but angry*): Well, I am surprised that Fred is so upset. I'm the one who should be cracking up. He started an affair with a technician in his building. I found out and told him to choose between her and me. He claims he chose me but I have witnesses who can prove he's been sleeping with the very same lady at least once a week. I want no part of our relationship.

FRED: But you're being so unreasonable. You could lose all that we've worked for. And think of the children. I still love you and the kids.

Fred and Donna faced a decision that is rarely easy to make. Despite the position she took in front of Fred, Donna revealed that she felt "close to cracking," that she did not know what would be best for her and the children but desperately wanted to make the right move.

Even partners who have come to despise each other will often hesitate to separate. One way to reduce the pain and increase the chances of finding the best solution is to employ problem-solving skills. Defining the problem then becomes relatively simple. The next step for Donna and Fred was to generate solutions on a Couple Crisis form.

Couple Crisis Form

Problem: Whether to separate.	
Possible solutions	Whose idea
1. Fred gives up his lover.	Fred
2. Fred leaves the home for two months while we take part in couple therapy.	Donna
3. We stay together, but get couple therapy.	Fred
4. Donna agrees to forgive and forget.	Fred
5. We file for a legal divorce.	Donna

(continued on next page)

6. Donna, without legal prejudice, leaves Fred and the kids for three months.	Donna
7. Donna goes back to work and Fred discontinues his affair while we get couple therapy.	Donna

Donna and Fred were able to generate a number of solutions to their problem; but the difficult task was agreeing on which one to choose. Both felt ambivalent and confused about what the future would hold no matter what solution they chose. They needed to do some careful soul-searching – alone – to understand the consequences of each choice.

Donna's problem-solving: Donna singled out the solution she most wanted to evaluate in detail: "We file for a legal divorce." She would then do the same for the remaining solutions that interested her.

The advantages and disadvantages Donna saw for the first solution are summarized below; they are categorized according to the seven important aspects of life. (These appear in the left-hand column.)

Couple Crisis Evaluation

Solution to consider:		
I file for a legal divorce.		
Dimension	**Advantages**	**Disadvantages**
A. The children	We will stop fighting in front of them. The situation will be clearer. We will stop disagreeing over how to discipline them. Fred is seldom at home now anyway. Fred could visit them regularly.	It's better that they live with both of us. Maybe I will be too upset by the separation to be a good mother. If I have to work to support myself and the children, I'll not have the time to be a good mother.

(continued on next page)

(continued)

B. My emotions	I am so angry and hurt, I don't want to live with Fred anymore.	I'll be all alone.
		I'll be depressed.
		I'll feel I'm a failure.
		People will judge me.
	I don't think I love Fred enough to forgive him.	I'll be letting the children down as a parent and I'll be giving them less security.
	Fred started withdrawing from our marriage at least four years ago.	
		My life will end.
	It's better that I face being alone now at thirty-four than when I'm older.	Perhaps I still love Fred.
C. Financial situation and possessions	A divorce lawyer told me that I have grounds for support.	Fred's practice is now losing money and he has made bad investments: I don't know where the support money will come from.
	Fred can keep the house if he gives me half the furniture and lump sum payment.	I will have to start work immediately.
		I hate to have to leave my house and to divide up our possessions.
D. My partner	Fred has wanted a younger woman since our last child was born.	Fred will miss the kids.
		Fred is afraid of not having enough money.
	Fred will survive because his work and amorous adventures have always come first with him.	Fred won't like the gossip our separation will cause.
		Fred's parents will give him a rough time because they like me.

(continued on next page)

		Fred would prefer to hold onto me as a wife, but have an open marriage.
E. Physical health	I'm feeling fine now. I should make a move now, while I still have the energy to start a new job.	I've been losing sleep and suffering from a nervous stomach and am smoking more. It will be hard on me if I'm sick when I'm on my own.
F. Legal	The lawyer said the separation and divorce will be simple procedures.	Fred may battle or contest my legal actions. I hate to use lawyers.
G. Other	I will not be the only one to experience separation and divorce; my sister and best friend have gone through the same experience.	My parents will be depressed. I don 't look forward to trying to meet someone new. With three kids, who would want me? How will our friends react?

Donna reported: "I see much more clearly now what I'm going through. I feel much less confused. Maybe therapy or an open marriage would work but I seriously doubt it. Our situation has gone on for so long that neither of us is able to turn back. I feel much too hurt and angry to forgive and forget. I'd much rather start afresh. I'm very afraid of what it will be like to be on my own with the children, but in many ways Fred has been an absent father since I was pregnant with our youngest child."

Fred's problem-solving: Fred felt ambivalent and confused as to which solution best suited him. He still felt strongly attached to Donna but as a friend and the mother of his children, not as a lover. He was very much in love with his most recent lover, who was pressuring him to let Donna have the children so that she and Fred could establish a new life together.

He was also concerned that his tight financial situation would not survive the support of two households. Finally, he asked that Donna help him arrive at a decision.

The subsequent meeting was filled with tears, accusations, remorse and promises. Donna informed Fred that she wanted a one-year trial separation, to be negotiated by their lawyers. Fred acquiesced, but stated he sincerely hoped that after one year they could find a way to still be together.

Fred and Donna and their two lawyers arrived at an agreement that did not demand a court appearance. The three children would live in a new apartment with Donna. Fred was to have the children from Saturday night to Sunday night. He was also able to visit them at times convenient to both him and Donna. The size of support payments, however, was more difficult to establish. Donna's lawyer convincingly demonstrated that she would need at least $1,200 a month to survive without a job for the immediate future and with three young children to support. But $1,200 a month was more than half of Fred's income. At first he balked at selling the large, expensive house that was in his name; but he finally agreed that he had no choice. As agreed in their original marriage contract, Donna was awarded all the appliances and half the furniture. They agreed that if either did not want to return to the marriage once the year was over, the other would accept an uncontested legal divorce.

Within a week of Donna and the children's departure, Fred moved into his lover's apartment; within two months the house was sold. Donna "made it through the first four months of shock" with the help of a therapist. Within ten months, she was working four mornings a week as a dental assistant. She dated occasionally, but was "not interested in any commitments now, or perhaps ever."

Fred was unpredictable with the children, and Donna found raising them alone very demanding. During the first six months, the two oldest blamed Donna for Fred's failure to visit on weekends, and they often accused her of being responsible for the separation. However, once she found a reliable baby-sitter, a fifty-year-old widow who lived in the same apartment building, "things looked up considerably."

At the end of the year, Donna and Fred agreed to file for divorce; but their demands led to a legal battle. Fred was feeling the strain of financing two households and petitioned for Donna's earnings to be subtracted from the total support payments. The judge accepted the plea; however, he decided that Fred was to reimburse Donna for babysitting and job-training expenses.

The confusion and ambivalence Fred and Donna felt during their marital crisis is commonplace. There is no magic formula that spares couples these painful days, months and even years, but a clear understanding of some of the options open to couples facing separation and divorce can help them make better decisions.

Option One: Consult a competent couple counsellor. Many couples believe that marriage counsellors are interested only in keeping partners together. However, helping a couple to divorce constructively is as important as helping a couple improve their relationships. Counsellors want the best for all parties concerned, and couples who seek counsellors during and after separation diminish the depression, low self-esteem, fighting and psychological effects on the children.

Option Two: Use problem-solving skills to reach rational decisions. During a crisis over the future of an intimate relationship, emotions are invariably intense. If reason is not brought to bear on the problem, emotions will dominate the decision making, and partners and children may suffer from the results. For example, hate and anger can lead one or both partners to favor retaliation: "You'll never see the children." "I'll take you for every penny you have."

Fear of being alone, on the other hand, can lead one or both partners to discount the possibility of separation despite the pains of staying together and the obvious disadvantages for the children. A careful evaluation of the rational and emotional advantages and disadvantages of each option will lead to a better long-term decision.

Option Three: Keep the well-being of your children at heart; but do not assume that staying together is the best option for them. A disturbed marital relationship and destructive separation can leave lasting scars on children; years later, they may experience guilt, depression, low self-esteem and hatred for one or both parents. They may exhibit behavioral problems, learning difficulties and confusion over sexual identity. However, if two parents maintain a positive parental relationship with their children, the negative consequences of separation and divorce can be greatly reduced or eliminated. For children, a constructive parental separation can be a much better experience than a destructive marriage.

Option Four: Couple therapy works for some couples. Fred and Donna put marital therapy on the list of possible solutions to their crisis; but Donna felt it was too late to repair the damage. However, if they had entered marital therapy during Donna's third pregnancy, when the partnership began to fall apart, there may have been a positive result. However, Fey and Wayne decided that couple therapy was worth a try. After reaching a new agreement on the "openness" of their relationship, Fey and Wayne used their survival strategies to renew their decision to stay together and to improve the quality of their relationship.

Option Five: Consider trial separation. Xavier and Huguette consulted our clinic on Xavier's insistence. Huguette wanted to separate, but Xavier begged her to reconsider.

Huguette, thirty-eight, worked as a public-health nurse on a large interdisciplinary team. Xavier, thirty-seven, was an unemployed steelworker. They had two sons and one daughter between the ages of fourteen and eighteen. In the past four years of their nineteen-year relationship, Huguette had increasingly felt the need to live on her own. She and her husband disagreed on many issues. She felt he was more conservative than she with regard to disciplining the children, leisure-time activities, trips, the openness of their marriage and financial planning. She also felt that Xavier had not looked for a job hard enough since he had been laid off eighteen months earlier.

Xavier agreed with almost all Huguette's opinions, but he felt their relationship deserved another chance. Huguette was willing to take part in couple therapy, provided that they live under separate roofs for one year, and that they have weekly "couple sessions" to improve communication with each other and with their children. Moreover, Huguette wanted Xavier to realize that just because they were in couple therapy she may still be interested in separation later on. Xavier accepted her conditions willingly.

Huguette moved out with the children and had her chance to try a new, more independent lifestyle. During the year, she enjoyed several intense relationships with men other than her husband and learned a great deal. Xavier did not date other women. Huguette found that the children treated her as the "bad" parent when her husband was absent; yet, when all five family members had lived under the same roof, Huguette and the children would usually be united against Xavier.

Despite the challenge of being a single parent, Huguette was very pleased with her newly won freedom. She was especially proud to have discovered that loneliness and financial stress were surmountable problems. She noticed that Xavier had also changed. He had become more open about his feelings and listened more actively.

Huguette realized that she still wanted to have a life with Xavier and agreed to move back in with him if he was willing to renegotiate their marriage contract to include joint ownership of all property. Xavier had found part-time employment and with new self-confidence welcomed her return.

Option Six: Obtain legal and financial advice. When the stability of their relationship is threatened, partners suddenly come to realize to what extent many of the legal and financial dimensions of their relationship have been taken for granted. Overnight, these become sources of great anxiety. Few events in our culture are more distressing than two people fighting in a divorce court over the legal or financial particulars of a separation. Yet, both partners should engage an experienced legal and financial advisor to answer the following questions:

1. What exactly does our marriage contract specify?
2. Given the nature of our crisis, what could be the grounds for divorce?
3. What financial arrangements can we expect?
4. Who will keep the house and furniture?
5. What child-custody arrangement would be best for us?

How to Survive a Separation or Divorce

Here are some of the problems and solutions that can reduce the pain of separation and divorce:

Problem One: Societal prejudices. Although marital breakup is increasingly commonplace, our culture continues to foster prejudices about separation and divorce. Partners who accept these prejudices only make their own lives more miserable.

"Because we divorced, we must be wicked, sick or sinful." Certain segments of society continue to criticize couples who divorce. Instead of trying to fight these attitudes, partners would do better to ask the following questions: "Is it really too late to save the relationship?" "If so, what can we all learn from the situation?" "How can we be good parents despite the separation?" "How can we approach the breakdown of the relationship in a constructive manner?"

"Separation and divorce are more harmful to the children than staying together in the relationship." Maintaining a relationship at all costs is not the answer. Children fare best when both partners are available and loving.[9] A constructive separation can be better for the children than a destructive marriage.

"My life will end when we part." Many partners, especially those who do not desire the separation, believe that there is no life after divorce. However, people who take active steps to rebuild their lives prove to be much happier within a year of the separation than they were during the year before it.

Problem Two: Powerful emotions. Partners invariably experience very powerful emotions during and after a separation:

Depression. A drop in self-esteem, optimism, *joie de vivre* and energy affects most people who separate, even if the partners want to split. A professional therapist can help restore damaged confidence and create a new sense of well-being. New friends, new activities and any other active steps to build a new life will help combat depression.

Anger. Many people feel a great deal of hostility toward their partner during and after separation. For some couples the hostility starts with the separation process; for others, the hostilities have much deeper roots.

Some people believe that the angry person should express his/her anger and hostility openly to the partner, with no holds barred, providing no one is physically injured. Others recommend that partners suppress their negative emotions to "remain the best of friends" throughout all eventualities. However, the most effective strategy falls between these two extremes.

Clearly, people should get in touch with what provokes their anger. The self-exploration questions described in Chapter Eight can help in this task. But the more one partner attacks the other, the more likely it is the distance and hatred between them will grow.

One partner in each of the three couples we have met in this chapter was very angry at the other: Donna at Fred; Phyllis at Milton; and Xavier at Huguette. It is understandable that they would want to attack, punish, criticize and hurt their partners, but through self-exploration they could discover what exactly makes them so angry and understand precisely what they feel.

It is unwise to keep anger bottled up, but there are constructive ways to express it openly. Before expressing anger directly to your partner, answer the following question. "If I tell my partner what I think of her/him, what will I gain and what will I lose?" Angry partners often anticipate benefits from expressing hostile feelings, such as feeling better or getting back at him/her for what he/she did. But they can anticipate losses: "He will be less interested in co-operating with me" or "The children will be hurt again by our fighting" or "She will try to get back at me by making my life more difficult."

Most couples will have difficulty maintaining a friendship after parting company, but they should never be enemies. Hostile partners suffer more complicated and more costly divorce proceedings. Moreover, the innocent bystanders, the children, will be harmed more by parents at war than by parents who separate as constructively as possible.

Loneliness. Many partners, especially those who did not initiate the separation, find solitude the worst consequence of the experience. Some prefer to live with a person they hate than to be alone, so they may allow a painful relationship to continue long after it should have ended. Others avoid loneliness by jumping immediately into a new relationship, with little regard for its suitability. Partners fear solitude for reasons that reflect their backgrounds and life experiences, yet, much to the surprise of many recently separated couples, the fear of solitude is often worse than solitude itself.

Newly separated partners should try to understand what it is about being alone that is so painful. The experience can often lead the individual to pleasantly surprising self-knowledge, which almost invariably improves one's ability to build a more satisfying new life. Friends, colleagues, family, single-parent groups and professionals can all be valuable helpmates while an individual slowly adjusts to being "alone."

Ambivalence and confusion. That most people feel disoriented during and immediately following a separation is not surprising, as marital breakup causes an upheaval in all areas of life: parenting, emotions, finances, careers and social life. Some families regard the separated person as a failure, as an embarrassment reflecting badly on themselves. Religious institutions and public agencies also can be judgmental.

Many questions, never raised before, suddenly face the separated person and accumulate with amazing rapidity: When will I eat? Where will I eat? What will I do tonight? Where will I go for vacation? Where will the money come from? What if I'm sick? The day-to-day, predictable routine is gone.

Few relationships are made up solely of love or hatred. A person who feels betrayed by his/her partner's request for a separation can feel very confused and depressed when hatred and love conflict. Some declare war on their former partner to avoid the feelings of ambivalence: "I would rather shut out my loving feelings. It hurts me less to hate than to love."

Problem Three: The children. Children are very vulnerable to conflict between parents. Concerned parents can considerably reduce the impact of marital breakdown on the children by anticipating the problems raised in "Troubleshooting Guide for Separating Parents." (See p. 219.)

Partners must remember that what counts most is that the children receive consistent loving and companionship from at least one parent. The sooner parents can put their differences behind them, the sooner they can provide a healthy environment for their children's new lives.

Problem		Possible Solutions
Living arrangements	1. With whom do the children live?	Consider what's best for the children. Ask for their opinion.
	2. What will the visitation rights be?	The children should see their other parent often and regularly. Visits should be predictable. Neither parent should make a habit of cancelling them.

(continued on next page)

(continued)

Single parent and problems of custody	3. Fatigue: you're never off duty.	Obtain the help of a babysitter. Take time off. Share activities with another single-parent family. Join a self-help group.
	4. Discipline: you're judge, jury and enforcer.	See 3, above. Follow courses on effective parenting or consult a professional for advice. Ensure that both parents exert discipline in a consistent manner. Do not allow children to play one parent off against the other.
New lovers and step-parents	5. Children respond with hostility: "You're the traitor."	Explain to the children why you want and need a new partner. Explain that your finding a new partner does not mean you love the children less. Read *The Boys' and Girls' Book About Divorce.*[9]
	6. Conflicts between your new partner and your children	Try to be a mediator between your new partner and your children.

Some of the problems faced by separated parents occur immediately following the separation; others do not appear for six months or more, or after one partner remarries. The "Troubleshooting Guide for Separating Parents" summarizes the most frequent problems couples face. Each problem can be solved in many ways; here is just a sampling of the solutions.

Troubleshooting Guide for Separating Parents

Problem: The Children's Feelings	Possible Solutions
1. "Nobody loves me."	Explain why you are separating. Impress upon them that it is not their fault. Tell them you love them as much as ever. Be loving and available.
2. "I'll be all alone."	Develop living arrangements whereby they can enjoy the sufficient company of both parents. Both parents express love to the children. Both parents behave lovingly to the children.
3. "I want you to stay together."	Explain why it is not possible for both to stay together. Explain that you are not parting because you love the children any less.
4. "I hate you for separating."	Do not fight in front of the children. Do not use the children to spy on your former partner. Do not use your children as go-betweens. Do not use your children to retaliate against your former partner. Tell the children you are sorry they hate you, because both of you love them very much.

Problem Four: Finances. Following a divorce or separation, both partners usually experience a decline in their standard of living. Maintaining two households is inevitably more costly than one household supported by the pooled resources of two working partners. Women are particularly vulnerable to financial hardship following a separation.

Even though women now enjoy greater educational and employment opportunities, they usually receive less pay than men for the same work. Since the separated woman usually has children living with her, it is she who must carry most of the financial and parenting burdens. Despite legislation to provide financial assistance in rearing her children, the single mother has no guarantee of support. Most men continue to default on their support payments.

Moreover, divorced women tend to stay single longer than divorced men, who remarry sooner and more often than divorced women, often to a woman considerably younger than the previous mate. Unfortunately, custody of the children and the attendant financial responsibilities often stand in the way of a woman's remarriage.

There are no easy solutions to the financial problems of separation. Financially stressed partners should seek emotional support from friends, family members, social agencies and single parents. Single mothers may also benefit from a number of financial strategies available to them.[10]

Problem Five: The new social identity. Most newly separated people are surprised and confused when colleagues, friends, family members and institutions treat them differently because they are suddenly single. Separation or divorce imposes a change in social identity particularly for women. Some find that their female friends become threatened: they view the new divorcée as a potential competitor for their mates. Male friends may treat the divorcée coolly: "I don't want to make my own partner jealous." Or seductively: "Let me help you deal with your loneliness." Social-service agencies and day-care centers are less generous to single mothers and their children than to fathers who have custody of the children.

Both men and women notice that many of their old friends are so locked into the "couple mentality"that they hesitate to invite them over once they are separated: "Foursomes are more fun than threesomes." This insensitivity only makes it harder for the separated individual to adjust to her/his new life.

One of the most demanding tasks that faces the newly separated person is building a new social life that includes friends of both sexes. Many are surprised by how much their old partnership protected them from the problems of socializing. Suddenly, they must relearn socializing skills, learn how and where to meet potential new partners, how to be interesting, how to choose new companions well, and how to decide what type of relationship to pursue once they have found a suitable mate. Some welcome the challenge of the new freedom; others are intimidated by the prospect of developing new intimate relationships. Many never mastered these social skills or are insecure because the "dating scene" has changed radically since they were single.

Solutions For the New Single

Patience is the most important ingredient in adjusting to being "single" or a "single parent." Begin by discounting such romantic notions as: "All my problems will be solved if I can meet the one right person" or "I will be happy only if I fall in love again." Coming to terms with one's new status involves creating a rewarding new – and single – lifestyle. Courses on how to be single successfully are becoming increasingly popular; self-help books can also help rebuild personal confidence and a positive, outgoing attitude.

Since the disintegration of the extended family, the modern couple has suffered from a lack of societal support. Separated couples are particularly vulnerable, as they experience the double loss of moral and financial support from both their former partners and society. The development of new social-support systems is essential to the survival of the newly single person, for, in our society, the number of persons who have gone through at least one divorce will soon outnumber those who have not. Single-parent groups and clubs for the divorced that encourage friendships as well as the evolution of new couples are needed until society changes its attitudes toward divorced partners. One day, it is hoped, society will appropriate resources and a more welcoming environment for divorced and separated men, women and parents.

13

What's Next? Options Open to Couples

Whatever stage your relationship is at, you will want to consider your next step. A summary of the options available follows, and factors you might consider in deciding "what's next" are discussed throughout this chapter.

1. Both you and your partner try to change your relationship with the help of survival strategies.
2. One partner tries to change the relationship with the help of survival strategies.
3. If your relationship has problems but is not yet in trouble, take a preventive survival course.
4. If you are in distress, seek out couple therapy.
5. If you and your partner have sexual problems, seek out sex therapy.
6. If you and your partner are not sure you want to remain a couple, seek the advice of a consultant to help you make the best decision possible.
7. If you want to separate, seek the aid of a consultant to arrange a constructive separation.
8. Strengthen your support groups by improving your relationships with family and friends or by joining a self-help group.
9. Do not do anything – either the relationship is fine or it is not time for a change.
10. If you are in doubt about the status of the relationship, try a couple checkup.

Should We Attempt to Change Our Relationship With the Aid of Survival Strategies?

If you are not yet experiencing tensions in your relationship, you may still want to strengthen or enrich your relationship. If you decide to use survival strategies, both of you should read and discuss this book. You need not see eye-to-eye on all points, but it will be important for you to agree on where and how to start to change your relationship.

Where to start: Each partner should jot down the answers to four questions:

1. What are the strengths of our relationship? (Sample answers: I am proud of our children and how we have raised them. I think we have a wonderful sex life. I feel understood and supported by my partner.)
2. What are the problems or conflicts that we have not been able to resolve satisfactorily? (Sample answers: We don't agree on finances. I feel the need for more love.)
3. What would I like to achieve through change? (Sample answers: Improved sexual relations. A more equal sharing of work. Resolution of our differences over extramarital sex.)
4. What survival strategies are most important for us to master? (You may choose a single strategy, several or all of them.)

Once you have answered these questions, exchange notes. Again, you need not see eye-to-eye on every question; what counts is that you develop a workable plan. The important thing is to tackle one problem at a time; start with the easiest. Examining your lists should lead you into a discussion of which problem you think would be easiest to solve.

You may have trouble deciding which skills to learn first. Any one of the eight survival strategies could be a good starting point, depending on your needs and strengths as individuals and as a couple. Usually, however, listening and speaking skills are tackled first, because without these skills, the learning and the practice of all the other skills is difficult:

love-enhancement and problem-solving techniques require a knowledge of self-disclosure and listening skills. Negotiation, fair fighting, sexual satisfaction, fair division of work and resolution of needs for independence all hinge on each partner's ability to communicate.

You may find it helpful to use this book in two parts. The first half covers the skills that can bring out the positive aspects of a relationship; the listening, self-disclosure and effective expression of love and sexuality skills can all be viewed as building blocks of a relationship. The skills described in the second part of the book are valuable for ironing out problems in a relationship. It is usually wiser to strengthen the positive areas before tackling the areas of conflict. The patience and good faith required to resolve problems effectively will only be sufficiently strong if the skills described in the first half of this book are already strong.

How to start: Once you have decided where to start, try to agree on how you plan to change. For example, if you have chosen to start on speaker-listener skills, make sure you both interpret Chapter Three in the same way. Reread it together and discuss each section. Focus on each rule and exercise suggested, discussing what each means to you. What time commitment are you prepared to make? Remember, the mastery of any one skill takes practice. Some couples find that fifteen minutes a day works well; others find that one-hour sessions two or three times a week are more effective. Find a time pattern that best suits your needs and routine.

How long will it take? This question is impossible to answer. Clearly, if you and your partner have already mastered several survival strategies, it is likely you will be able to make improvements in other areas quite quickly. Motivation is a crucial factor: if you and your partner really want to improve your relationship, you will probably be able to develop the necessary skills relatively quickly, even if you are starting from scratch.

If you find that, as you go along with your self-help plan, you cannot effect changes as quickly as you had hoped, a consultant might be able to help by giving you a couple checkup and offering suggestions on what you could do next.

What Should I Do If My Partner Does Not Want to Participate?

Do not be surprised if your partner does not show the same interest as you do. Not all partners believe that their relationship can be improved; not all people believe that consultation with an outsider is worthwhile. This can be very frustrating for the partner who is motivated to change. However, reluctant partners can often be interested in reading a book or visiting a consultant if they understand that it is an opinion their partner is after, not necessarily a commitment to change.

If the keener partner says, "Read this book, it will improve our relationship," or "Let's go see Dr. A, she will help us change our relationship," the reluctant partner may become defensive. You must ask your partner if he/she thinks your relationship needs help; do not assume that you know the best way to proceed: "I would like to know what you think of this book," or "I would like us to go for a couple checkup," is not asking your partner to make a commitment to change but merely to try something out so you can discuss it together.

If this diplomatic tack does not work, return to the problem-solving strategies in Chapter Six and follow the procedure for examination of a problem you face as an individual: "I want to do X to improve our relationship and my partner does not. What should I do now?" Some possible choices of action are:

1. Tell your partner how you see the situation.
2. Start a fight.
3. Attempt to get your partner into a problem-solving discussion.
4. Have an affair.
5. Seek an opinion from a consultant without the presence of your partner.
6. Try to learn some of the survival skills alone.
7. Seek a separation.

You must look for a solution that fits your particular situation.

226

Should We Attend a Couple-Enrichment Program?

Courses designed to help partners improve their chances of survival and to learn skills useful in a relationship have been attended by hundreds of thousands of North American couples.[5] Most of these programs are designed for couples who are not yet in trouble. They vary in the number of participants (usually between eight and fifty), length (most are twelve to thirty-six hours), cost, type of training the leaders have had, the skills taught and whether there is a spiritual or religious element.

Some, such as the very popular Marriage Encounter program, use mainly nonprofessional group leaders and concentrate on teaching couples to develop the positive aspects of their relationship. Other programs, such as the popular Minnesota Couples Communication Program, are conducted by professionals and attempt to teach couples how to bring out the positive side of their relationship, how to solve problems and how to deal with conflict. This type of program always begins with a two- to three-hour couple checkup to determine the couple's needs. This checkup is very valuable. Programs offered by religiously affiliated groups, such as Marriage Encounter or Divorce Encounter, generally carry out no initial assessment of a couple.

Do We Need Couple Therapy?

Couples who fight a lot, who feel estranged, who have great difficulty communicating or who feel overpowered by unresolved problems may want to consult a professional. Objectives, number of sessions and type of consultant can vary greatly. Couple therapy differs from couple-enrichment programs: therapy is usually designed to help couples who are currently in distress; enrichment programs are rarely equipped to help couples in acute distress or close to separation.

Couple therapy will occasionally help a couple to learn the survival skills, but usually sessions discuss and resolve their specific problems. Most enrichment programs are designed to help a couple develop general skills, not to discuss specific problems.

Do We Need Sex Therapy?

If you decide to improve the sexual dimension of your relationship through sex therapy, both you and your partner should become involved: both can learn to understand the problem and how to modify your sexual behavior as a couple, with the help of a trained professional.

Do We Need Professional Help to Make a Decision?

You may not be sure which alternative best suits your situation. Consultation with a professional can be very helpful while you are trying to decide whether you should stay together or separate and how to proceed most constructively. If you reach an impasse in your plans to help your relationship, a consultant can help you decide what you should do next.

Do We Need to Consult a Professional to Arrange a Constructive Separation?

Couples who decide to separate invariably face emotional, intellectual, social, parental, legal and financial problems. But those who receive separation counselling tend to reduce the length and severity of their own and their children's problems. Separation counselling can also help each partner learn from the experience so that their future life, whether alone or with a new partner, will be more fulfilling.

Do We Need to Develop Stronger Social Support?

Many communities have organized groups in which single parents lend each other support. These self-help groups can provide an individual or couple with essential support that used to come from the extended family. Your local social-service agency should be able to tell you about what services are available in your community. Individuals and couples can, of course, develop valuable channels of understanding and support by strengthening relationships with family members and friends.

Do We Really Need to Change?

After reading this book, you may find that you understand your relationship better than before. You may also decide that, although you would like to change your relationship in some way, now is not the time to do it. A couple who feels that their relationship has many positive aspects and few painful or unpleasant dimensions may not want to disturb the status quo. One or both partners might feel certain changes are needed but no modifications should be made right away. Financial insecurity, illness, pregnancy or risk of violence may deter partners from rocking the boat. The motivated partner who cannot convince her/his mate to begin a relationship improvement project – or even to read this book – might decide to wait for a better moment to broach the subject again.

Should We Have a Couple-Therapy Checkup?

Couples should not take their relationships for granted. Although intimate relationships are very complex, there are certain typical patterns that can be recognized and understood. Trace the history of your relationship and pick out the stress points or key events for you as a couple. Couples frequently mentioned:

1. Decision to get married.
2. When the honeymoon was over.
3. Pregnancy.
4. The birth of a child.
5. Unemployment.
6. Change of job.
7. Extramarital affairs.
8. Illness.
9. Working together.
10. Moving.
11. Forced separation (work, study or health-related).
12. When the children left home.
13. Retirement.

Couples can anticipate that at one or several of these points, the stress level on their relationship will increase. A strong intimate relationship can be of help against life's stresses. However, a stable, healthy relationship is not a limitless resource; but it may not send noticeable distress signals for months or even years.

By regularly taking stock of their relationship in a "checkup," a couple can avoid irreversible damage. Although there are ways of undoing years of damage, replenishing a relationship's resources can get more difficult as time goes on. A couple checkup by the couple alone or with a professional is an evaluation of each partner's view of the couple's strengths and problems. A couple who reviews their situation every three or six months can keep track of how balanced the relationship is and how well each partner's needs are being satisfied.

A successful intimate relationship is a precious thing, well worth the time and energy invested to protect it. Many couples have found that with a little practice and a few new skills, maintenance and improvement of their life together is not only challenging, but fun.

Bibliography

1. Lasswell, M., Lobsenz. M.M. (1980): *Styles of Loving.* New York: Ballantine.
2. Gottman, J., Notarius, C., Gonso, J., Markman, H. (1976) *A Couple's Guide to Communication.* Champaign, Illinois: Research Press.
3. Masters, W. H., & Johnson, V. E. (1966). *Human sexual response.* Boston: Little, Brown & Co.
4. Masters, W. H. & Johnson, V. E. (1970). *Human sexual inadequacy.* Boston: Little, Brown & Co.
5. Wright, J., Sabourin, S. (1985). *Helping Couple's Survive: A socio-cognitive approach to marital intervention. A Manual for Therapists and Teachers.* Montreal: Les Editions Consult Action.
6. Bach, C. R., Wyden, P. (1968). *The intimate enemy.* New York: Avon Books.
7. MacLeod, L., Cadieux, A. E. (1980). *Wife battering in Canada: The vicious circle.* Ottawa: Canadian Advisory Council on the Status of Women.
8. O'Neill, N., O'Neill, G. (1972). *Open Marriage: A new lifestyle for couples.* New York: Evans & Co. Inc.
9. Gardner, R. (1970). *The Boys' and Girls' Book About Divorce.* New York: Bantam.
10. Napolitane, C., and Pellegrino, V. (1977). *Living and loving after divorce,* Toronto: McClelland and Stewart.